The Apocalypse of Desire

Essays in Mimesis

Luca Luchesini

Contents

Introduction

This book collects the essays I wrote using mimetic theory as interpretation tool in a number of fields ranging from the genesis of morals, the nature of power, the interpretation of modern history and West-Middle East relations. I therefore decided to regroup and re-edit them into a single edition to highlight the theory power in a more systematic way than it appears in the single essay and as a tribute to René Girard, whose books sounded to me no less than pure revelation. The core finding of Girard is that desire is what ultimately drives human action, and this desire is literally built around nothing, or better, it has no specific and real object that can fulfill it. That is the "ontological" precondition that allows people to change and imitate each other desires and this at once amazing and scaring feedback game is the root of both the best human achievements and the worst disasters.

The first two essays of the collection explore the insights that mimetic theory provides in explaining the birth and development of human nature. "The righteously mimetic Mind" delves more with the development of morals, both in early mankind and at individual level while "Power, Crowds, Violence and Desire" goes more in detail about the role of mimesis in the development of power structures. The third essay, "Desire and the West" applies mimetic theory to the interpretation of the historical changes happened in the modern era. Finally, the last essay, "Rival Brothers", applies mimetic theory to the current status of East-West relations and gives some practical example on how mimetic theory can help in everyday life.

The Righteously Mimetic Mind - Morality, Politics and Human Development between J.Haidt and R.Girard

Introduction

This essay connects the dots between "The Righteous Mind", the recent success of Jonathan Haidt about the evolutionary foundations of morality and mimetic theory developed by René Girard around the key concepts of imitative desire and scapegoating.

The two authors come from very different backgrounds and yet they share a deep interest in researching the process that created mankind.

A Catholic literary theorist turned anthropologist, René Girard (born 1924) published in 1973 "Violence and the Sacred" where he explained the role of imitative desire and unanimous violence against isolated victims in the birth of primitive religions, myths and rituals. He later extended his research to biology and evolution to research the appearance of the scapegoat mechanism in animal and pre-human species, attracting more than one suspicion from the Roman Catholic establishment of excessive rationalization of religion. On the other hand, Jonathan Haidt, a Jewish liberal atheist somehow traveled in the opposite direction: starting from a liberal, rational and evolutionary cultural background he discovered all along his research in developmental psychology the multi-faceted nature of human morals, and he eventually rehabilitated religion as a distinctive feature of mankind, openly disagreeing with the "New atheist" view that sees religion as a bug in the evolution process of the human species.

For Haidt religion is no bug, indeed it plays a crucial role in keeping groups together albeit he concedes to his fellow atheists that there is no such thing as transcendence but only a psychological "self-transcendence".

Girard and Haidt also share a clear and rigorous style in the exposition of their views and they are both aware that their theories can have a revolutionary impact. The first two chapters provide a brief overview of Haidt thinking about the evolution and nature of morality and Girard theory of the origin of religion and culture. The chapter about mimetic theory begins with a "prelude" on the thinking of Elias Canetti, who is a precursor to both Girard and Haidt. In the third and fourth chapters we describe the common ground as well as the challenges that the two theories pose to each other. In the fifth chapter we list some of the implication of the two theories on current political and moral thinking, as both theories provide very valuable insight into human origins and behavior.

With a bit of hype, the works of Haidt and Girard might prove in humanities the equivalent of general relativity and quantum theory in the physical realm, that is two explanations not fully compatible yet invaluable in understanding a large part of our world.

Chapter 1 – Morality, Religion and Politics in Jonathan Haidt

Jon Haidt structures his work around three key concepts about morality. The first is that morality, far from being a purely rational construction, is instead the result of a very complex interplay between people, their environment and their genetic heritage. Our morals have been shaped and hard wired in our brains by hundreds of thousands of years of ever growing interaction, initially between small groups of people belonging to the same kin and then complex societies spanning whole countries and disparate ethnic groups. Rationality marks a very late appearance in this scale and while the vast majority of philosophers since the time of Plato has always claimed the supremacy of reason in defining our moral compass, Haidt tries to demonstrate that rational thinking actually serves as a lawyer to passions

As Hume said, rationality provides at best post-hoc justifications to our moral intuitions rather than steering passions in the wished direction based on some knowledge of a pre-existing truth. Starting from this assumption, Haidt then exposes his second key concept, the morality map, or the six main axes along which evolution has developed human morals, in order to maximize the effectiveness of human groups and societies at cooperating against internal and external threats and improving their overall condition. Finally, the third concept advocated by Haidt is that this groupish and biased morality that is able to both bind people together and blind them to the reasons of other competing groups is actually the best evolutionary adaptation that allowed the huge success of mankind. Our righteous minds allowed us to develop both aspects of our dual nature, the relentlessly selfish and competitive "chimp side" and at the same time the self-transcendent belonging to our group or "hive side".

Let's analyze this concepts more in detail, starting from the origin of morality in intuitions. To explain this, Haidt uses the elephant and rider metaphor, stating that the relationship between rationality and moral intuitions is like the one of a rider versus an elephant. The rider cannot actually steer the elephant exactly where he wants to, nor is the elephant staying idle waiting for the rider to give a direction. Rather, the elephant starts following his own course based on instinct, need, wish and intuition and the rider can only try to influence this course with some skillful commands and post-hoc directions. With this metaphor in mind, Haidt challenges with a strong amount of experimental evidence collected from both psychological and anthropological research the millennial Western view that morality is a rational construction carried out from our early childhood and based on the core avoid harm/do no harm experience.

On the experimental psychology front, Haidt demonstrates that in practical situations also well educated people of modern societies decide more on reputation, influence and intuition in choosing a specific moral behavior rather than cool reasoning. And by comparing Western societies to non-Western ones (or, more in general, modern societies versus pre-modern ones) Haidt shows with his own research the consistency and actually larger meaning of their moral systems once the social nature of morality is taken into account. In other words, in the West morality is meant mainly as a way to rationally determine the right and wrong in the interaction between single individuals.

On the contrary, in non-Western societies it is the main tool used to define one's position, duties and rights not only in individual transactions but also in the broader body of society and even the whole universe. From Plato to Kant and the recent

"Theory of Justice" of John Rawls, Western philosophy has always asserted that rationality should be the sole compass driving moral decisions, constantly struggling to dominate passions that always tend to take us astray from the path to virtue and happiness. And why would rationality be granted this primacy? According to Plato, for the very simple reason that only rationality could lead people to grasp truth and only founding our individual and collective decisions on truth can guarantee the happiness of the individual and the progress of society. Christianity bought big time the concept of "good rational truth" versus "bad passions", adding that beyond reason also grace was needed to attain virtue and happiness.

It is only with Hume that the role of passions and intuitions in shaping morality has been strongly re-asserted, with the British philosopher declaring rationality nothing more as a servant of the passions. Haidt elephant and rider model is much closer to Hume than Plato, so that reason may not actually be a mere servant to passions but rather it behaves like a lawyer or a very efficient press office agent, providing ex-post moral reasoning to our intuitions to win friends and allies and influence other people of the correctness of our behavior.

In short, moral reasoning provides first and foremost a social function and not a standalone compass of one's own spiritual elevation. It is very late in the evolution trajectory that the "rationality of the philosopher" appeared next to the "rationality of the lawyer", that is in the last few thousand years of a process started a few millions year ago with the appearance of the first hominids. And in the previous hundreds of thousands of years of evolution our "inner lawyer" has been developing a morality map that shaped our success as a species of highly efficient collaborative individuals.

The morality map is the second conceptual contribution of Haidt that we describe now in more detail. Jonathan Haidt derives the morality map from experiments in moral psychology, from his studies in cultural anthropology in India and Latin America and from the social theories of Emile Durkheim. The first observation is that modern societies where we live in the US and Europe are indeed quite WEIRD, used as acronym of Western, Educated, Industrialized, Rich and Democratic.

10

Without entering now into a cause-effect discussion, it is a fact that members of WEIRD societies tend to see the world (natural and social) as a collection of independent objects and not relationships. The moral concerns are mostly limited to questions of avoiding to harm, oppress or cheat other individuals.

It is also a measurable fact that outside of WEIRD societies other dimensions of morality exist, and these dimensions, in line with the thinking of Durkheim, see the family or the tribe as the basic unit of society and therefore value tradition, hierarchy and order much more than WEIRD societies.

Haidt then defines six main dimensions of morality, and for each of them a core value matched by its opposite non-value or evil. The six dimensions are: Care (harm), Fairness (cheat), Loyalty (betrayal), Authority (subversion) and Sanctity (degradation). These core values for Haidt are not the revelation of a God or innate in our "soul" since time immemorial, but are simply the result of the natural selection process to which also our minds have been subject.

Indeed, a mind responsive to Care (harm) emotional triggers is needed to effectively protect children. You also have to have a sense of fairness to be able to establish effective two way relationship, and when relationship encompass a group, then loyalty is crucial for the group to work properly and to avoid the free riders problem. As groups get larger they require complex hierarchies to run their organizations and this requires respect for authority and sensitivity to rank. Finally, groups and societies have to avoid contamination and contagion, first physically but then also in terms of social conflict diffusion and here is where Sanctity rules come to help.

Without a single one of these core features it would have been impossible for "evolved chimps" like us to assert ourselves as the world dominant species, so if we ask ourselves the question why our morality is engineered along these axes the answer from Haidt is in line with the anthropic principle: we are like this simply because otherwise we would not be here to ask ourselves the question and we would have instead before long succumbed to cave bears, bacteria and not least our own conflicts.

Obviously, being organized along these six moral axes does not mean that we all behave the same. A bit like the Kantian categories of perception tend to frame the way we produce our statements about reality, the moral dimensions of Haidt frame the way we produce our ethic judgments and the way this happens can vary widely at different latitudes and times. But according to Haidt at birth we are by no means a blank slate but rather a pre-wired palette that reacts and positions along these six directions shaped by hundreds of thousands of year of successful human evolution. In other words, innateness exists in the sense that we are organized in advance of experience but yet we have considerable freedom and society also has a considerable influence in defining our final position along this six-dimension space.

Haidt and his scholars have recently added a seventh axis to our moral compass, that is the Liberty (oppression) foundation. This appeared very late in the history of mankind (the first theorization of tyranny can be traced back to the Ancient Greeks, e.g. the "Heron" dialogue of Xenophon), but according to Haidt this can be traced back to the evolutionary process of preventing attempted domination and overthrow of "cheating alpha males" no longer perceived to serve the good of the group. In the last part of his work, Haidt tries to demonstrate the original intuition of Charles Darwin that morals appeared and evolved as the main tool to foster group selection.

The very notion of group selection is controversial within classic evolution theory, that asserts that evolution works at the individual level and prefers to talk about multi-level selection. Haidt does not provide conclusive evidence but rather what he calls favorable exhibits.

The first one is the observation that whenever the evolutionary process manages to solve the free-rider problem inevitably super-organism structures appear with dominant characteristics. The first example was the passage from viruses to cells, the last one the appearance of the modern corporation versus the single craftsman.

The second exhibit is the appearance in hominids of shared intentionality (now estimated to have happened around 6-700 thousands of year ago), that is the capability to share common goals and act in a coordinated way between the members of a group. To have a vivid example of shared intentionality, Haidt quotes research done comparing adult chimps with toddlers. Quite often, chimps outdo little babies at tasks involving individual ability like extracting food from boxes. On the other hand, chimps always fail against babies when reaching the goal requires doing something together, like carrying a log between two points.

The third exhibit is the observation that genes and culture from that point started to co-evolve, with individual more adapt to produce effective group behavior transmitting their genes more often and leading to even more cohesive and effective groups. Haidt eventually cites as last exhibit the proof that evolution can be fast, with pronounced changes happening in a species after just a few generations.

One may object that the examples that Haidt shows (chickens and foxes) are too much animal and too much driven in their evolution by external factors, namely the manipulation of man. On the other hand, mankind manipulation is also a factor of nature and again one cannot deny the overall acceleration that happened with mankind over the last few thousand years compared to the timescales of hundreds of thousands of years required by previous transitions.

In the last part of his book, Haidt explains the idea that morality is indeed a key success factor in evolution and that it actually serves the double purpose of binding and blinding human groups. The fact is, says Haidt, that humans are 90% chimp and 10% bee, that is selfish beings striving to belong to a bigger and nobler entity. People reach ecstasy when they are able to transition to the feeling of "being part of a whole". With a direct reference to Durkheim (and an indirect one to Canetti that I clarify later) Haidt identifies three ways by which people can reach this state: awe in nature, drugs, and social raves (e.g. sports, musical, religious and political rallies of any sort).

Again, Haidt tries to bring experimental evidence or at least exhibits to our nature, and he mentions the research around mirror neurons and oxytocin. But no matter what the underlying biological reason might be, it is a fact that morality does not generally prescribe an unconditional love and loyalty but rather more parochial binds, that is the allegiance with those with whom we share a more common fate and values, blinding us to the reasons and needs of other groups.

Just like Hegel did in his "Phenomenology of Mind", Haidt reserves the penultimate chapter of his "Phenomenology of Morals" to religion. Unlike Hegel, Haidt can afford to declare his atheism, but he agrees with Hegel that religion, far from being a bug is indeed a distinctive feature of mankind, putting himself against the views of the "New atheists".

According to the "New Atheists religion originates from the hypersensitive agent detection device, that is the tendency to imagine agents also where they are not easily recognizable. In other words, primitive men had to spot threats quickly and react even faster to survive so evolution favored individuals with better detection capabilities. However, this feature led our ancestors to seek for causes even where a direct agent was not immediately visible, like in natural phenomena. Spirits and gods were then invented and eventually myth and religion developed.

Haidt does not subscribe to this view and neither does mimetic theory. In anticipation of the next chapter, mimetic theory agrees with Haidt and Durkheim in placing a social phenomenon at the origin of religion, in particular the sacrifice of a scapegoat at the peak of a community crisis that is then rethought over time to form the basis of the myth narrative, including the myth of the creation of the world. Our ancestors did not sit around fire to speculate about gods, the structure of the universe and the best social organization. It was rather their increasing social interaction whose positive effects they attributed to external, divine forces that pushed them more and more to sit around fires and progressively refine community hierarchies and eventually the representations of myth.

For Haidt and mimetic theory religion is a feature far more than a bug, in particular the feature that above all contributed to elicit commitment and suppress or at least limit the free riders. After this long and inspirational journey between experimental psychology, philosophy and evolution, Haidt reserves the final paragraphs of his book to the reason that got him started, that is the extreme partisanship of current American politics. Equipped with his findings he tries to frame the debate between liberals and conservatives as a dialectic of yin and yang, acknowledging points from both sides (e.g. markets do make miracles as pointed out by libertarians and conservatives, yet governments must regulate corporations to limit the powers of these super-organisms) and even more important by reasserting the foundations of mutual legitimacy of each side.

Chapter 2 – The crowds of Canetti and the imitative desire of Girard

We start from the theory of crowds of Elias Canetti, because he starts where Jonathan Haidt ends his book. In his masterpiece treaty "Crowds and Power" Canetti describes the psychological experience that leads people to join a crowd, the classification of the different types of crowd, and the close relation between crowds and power. In the words of Haidt, Canetti lived and later rationalized a hive experience early in his youth years. In the quest for an explanation of his hive nature, Canetti has rejected the findings of contemporary psychoanalysis (he was one of the first readers of "Introduction to the psychology of masses" of Sigmund Freud) because the new science was failing to put the crowd instinct as a founding concept like the Oedipus.

Why do people have a compelling pulse to join crowds according to Canetti? Because they provide an antidote, albeit temporary, to the typical human trend of differentiation and take people back to a state where they are equal to each other and without any bound. People tend inexorably to differentiate, from any point of view: society progressively defines the role, responsibility and position of each individual within political and professional hierarchies, when it comes to knowledge each one of us keeps shaping a certain competence in a well-defined field and in our relations we evolve from the original, undifferentiated link of the newborn with the mother to the development of one's own and unique network of family and friends.

And yet, as much as this process is essential in shaping our own individuality in the search of fulfillment it is at the same time the first constraint to our desire of transcendence and immortality. By removing any external distinction and providing the instant experience of being part of a much bigger whole,

15

crowds fulfill, albeit temporarily, this basic desire of mankind. Canetti calls the discharge the moment in which a group of people dumps individuality and becomes behaving as a single entity in a crowd. It can be induced, as also Haidt recalls, with specific techniques like e.g. singing, marching or even the attack of an external force like anti-riot police. From this moment on, the crowd behaves and reacts as one single being until, at some point in time it erupts and every individual returns to its previous position in life and society.

Canetti then classifies crowds based on their dominant sentimental attitude and their spatial collocation: crowds can be baited against a specific enemy or class of enemies, or they can be unified by the movement toward a common goal (either real or ideal) or away from a common threat. Most often, crowds find balance when they can confront another opposing crowd (the double crowd) whereby the two entities, while trying to overrule each other, provide also the primary reason of being to each other. Double crowds typically apply to national and party rivalries, but also extend to the basic symbolic notions of the living and the dead or males and females. The parliamentary system eventually sublimates this dynamic by fixing the two crowds of the majority and the opposition and it regulates their clash in the vote mechanism. Moving to the symbolic plane, Canetti shows that the first elements that mankind had to master in its evolution like fire, the waters of seas, rivers and rain, the trees of the forests, the sands of the deserts or the herds of wild animals all had to some extent the distinct characteristic of crowds: they are made by many smaller elements, they can behave as a unity and become unstoppable, incorporating everything they find on their way.

Canetti does not explain in detail how the experience of these phenomena of natural crowds influenced the primitive man, however when it comes to the genesis of the crowd, Canetti observes that to start a crowd it is necessary to have a smaller group of people that can identify themselves with a goal and act as a catalyst for the bigger crowd to form, if the right environmental conditions arise. This catalyst is called the "crowd crystal" and is indeed the first structure that for Canetti appeared in primitive groups in the form of the pack. Based on the anthropological studies available in the 1950s, Canetti identifies four types of pack: the hunting pack, the war pack, the lamenting pack and the increase pack. These packs can mutually transform into each other.

The hunting pack and its hierarchy are similar to those of the animal world. It is only with mankind however that the war, increase and lamenting pack appear for the first time. While hunting packs are directed at animals and driven mainly by the need to procure food, war packs are directed exclusively at other rival human groups and can be triggered also by futile grounds of provocation. Hegel would say that these are the first distinctive human actions, and Haidt would probably agree that packs have been the first new social structures enabled by shared intentionality.

The hierarchy tasks evolve as well: the human leader must manage very precisely the booty allocation between pack members. Unlike in animals where after the hunt hierarchy translates simply in the respect of a fixed pecking order, hierarchies in people are always at risk of being challenged by the relentless action of desire and envy. The booty obtained in hunt and war helps also transforming the war pack into an increase pack, that is to say a group of people defined by some kind of ritual whose goal is the increase of the amount of cattle, food, slaves or any other good needed by the community.

No matter how victorious, some members of the community perished in action, and then the lamenting pack fulfills the double goal of at once re-asserting the unity of the survivors in their grief for the dead and establishing the mirror crowd of the dead to whom the perished members of the community are handed over. Of course, a pack lamenting the dead in battle can turn into a war pack and so on. Canetti also sees the birth of the lamenting pack as a way to discharge the psychological strain that the pain of the victims of the war/hunting pack creates, a kind of purification ritual for the winners. The lamenting pack is also the ground upon which every religion is built, and Canetti provides many examples of rituals that have arrived to this day both in Christianity and Islam.

While Canetti uses for the explanation of crowds an almost mathematical scheme with definitions, logical deductions and proof points, he approaches power with a very different perspective by analyzing the core mechanism of food processing and its associated organs, namely the hands and their extensions to grab the prey, the mouth to kill and crush it and the stomach and other hidden organs to digest it. According to Canetti the variety of forms that power has taken in human history with all its associated institutions, symbols and rituals ultimately rely on the core violence of the predator-prey relationship. Canetti identifies three founding elements of power: the Survivor who rules via Commands and establishes links between things with Transformations or metamorphosis.

The predator-prey relationship is experienced by people in the various forms of the hunting and warring packs that give birth to the figure of the Survivor. The Survivor is the one that came back alive and victorious from the hunt or the war, thereby establishing its power not only on the dead enemies but also on the dead friends. The more the dead in the battle, the more power is granted to the Survivor and the more his community is guaranteed to benefit from his leadership in increasing its rule among the neighboring groups. It is the Survivor who oversees how to split the loot among the pack: it is up to him to define who gets what, always following a very precise ritual that mimics the one used by the religious leader in managing the religious sacrifice. However, the paradox that arises is devilish: to cement his power, the Survivor needs to increase the crowd of the dead, and while the primary and explicit targets are indeed the enemies of the opposing crowds, there will be more and more casualties also among his own community. The harsh reality is that the Survivor power benefits from both types of death while the community at some point in time will see the cost-benefit balance enter into a crisis that can find a solution only in the self-destruction of the community or in the ousting of the ruler. We can find here maybe a precursor of the Liberty (oppression) axis investigated by Haidt.

When it comes to command, Canetti makes the crucial observation that command precedes language and is founded in the pre-human and cross-species interaction of the flight command, to which any prey obeys as soon as the presence or even the suspect of presence of the predator is detected. Canetti traces all subsequent evolutions of command to the threat of death. What is mankind adding to this basic interaction? In people, every command creates a feedback sting in those that receive it, a resentment to retaliate and transfer the very same command to someone else at a later date. It does not really matter how and when the transfer happens, neither if we can transfer back to those who gave us the initial command. The key point is to have the possibility to offload this reminder that eventually relies on a threat of punishment and a more or less explicit reminder of death. How to cure it? It is either the promise of a promotion (transform from slave and potential victim/prey to master and predator) or the discharge in a reversal crowd at the expense of the Survivor or in a broader sense the ruling class.

The third element introduced by power in the horizon of mankind is transformation. Transformation begins right during the hunt, where hunters feel the prey or mimic its sounds, smell and sights to better attract it into a trap. The preys and enemies enact every type of transformation to flee. And rulers learn to hide and conceal their true intention while at the same time simulating and impersonating different ones to defend and extend their power over the community. At the same time, rulers cannot help transforming space around them with cities, buildings, triumph arches and the like to mark their existence.

The connection between crowds and power is now clear. Deeply rooted in the violent origins of mankind, hunting and war packs lead to the emergence of the Survivor, who fulfills a triple role: he guarantees booty repartition, he ensures the increase of resources for the community and he is granted absolute power over the members of the community to eradicate with his arbitration any risk of disorder due to internal conflicts. Power needs crowds to assert itself and as object of its commands and this is counterbalanced by the fact that the crowd might rebel and become a toppling crowd where the rulers become the designated victims. This is leading to the paranoia of the powerful people, who typically see themselves surrounded by hostile crowds (be them people, animals, spirits, they are always persecuted by crowds). But crowds need power to keep them together and provide through the physical presence of their leaders the feeling of unity and harmony first perceived in the victorious battle. To achieve this, crowds are willing to confer to their rulers the right of death over their members as foundation of command.

The power of the king can continue as long as the increase of the community from pack to crowd is guaranteed, but increasing the well-being of the community implies a growing level of command that slowly builds up sting mass in that very same crowd until reversal crowds do away more or less violently with the existing order and build a new one. Power keeps seeding the roots of its own destruction, often a violent one.

In sum, Canetti starts from the hive experience of Haidt and eventually travels back to the dawn of mankind highlighting more the dark side or at least the dark roots of our civilized, moral society. If Haidt presents us with the final result of the six axis morals, Canetti reflects more on the gruesome process that led to its early development. And unlike Haidt, who strives to create a common ground between and beyond political rivalry and factiousness, Canetti does not see any path by which power struggling could transcend its violent origin. But unlike Haidt Canetti does not apply its findings to religion, even though he constantly intersects it in his reflection about crowds. It is then time to pass to mimesis or mimetic theory.

Mimetic theory has been developed by René Girard in the early 1960 first as a tool for literary critique and eventually as a full blown cultural anthropology framework. René Girard described mimetic desire in literature in his seminal work "Desire, Deceit and the novel", and later extended his research to the sacred and to primitive societies, openly acknowledging his debt to Canetti and Durkheim. For a systematic description I refer the interested reader to the first chapters of "Things hidden from the foundation of the world".

I do not give a precise definition of desire, I just note that it must not be mistaken with need (like the need for food and shelter) nor with instinct (which, taking for example the most famous one, the sexual instinct, is an internal drive with a clear and defined object that can satisfy it). Both needs and instincts have well defined objects and while people cannot survive long without taking proper care of needs, the same does not apply to instincts whose satisfaction can be postponed almost indefinitely without jeopardizing the basic living functions.

Desire does not have a specific object, in the sense that it can take any object as its content (a woman, a flag, a social position and so on). Desire is mimetic, that is people cannot help imitating each other's desires. We desire the most disparate things just because other people do it, regardless of their objective utility. So what? After all, this is exactly what all parents with small children know very well, without going to psychology classes. The value of mimetic theory is to be very consequent with the implications of the triangular nature of desire.

According to mimetic theory, there is no such thing as a direct link between the desired object and the one who desires, but there is always a third person, the mediator, to whom people look to know what to desire. Mediation of desire can in turn be classified in two categories, external and internal one. External mediation happens when the mediator is perceived as belonging to a complete different class by the one who desires and is therefore not perceived as a rival and this typically leads to positive emulation. This is what happens for example between an extraordinarily gifted teacher and his pupils, or between a saint and his followers. Internal mediation instead arises when the one who desires sees the mediator at the same level, with no special rights on the common desired object. If we are bound to crave the same objects and we see ourselves as equals, rivalry and conflict are inherent dynamics of human interaction.

Now, when we project that into Stone Age we need to figure out a mechanism to control rivalry if we do not want to run the risk of violent escalations that can lead to the self-destruction of the initial, fragile human communities. Mimetic theory identifies that in the scapegoat mechanism, whereby all the tensions are transferred to one member of the community and discharged via its elimination, with the perfect good faith of all the survivors that the victim is really guilty of all the evil that is ravaging the group. The victim can be human or animal and its elimination physical or symbolic. Over time mankind moved from the physical elimination of people to the symbolic expulsion of animals or things, albeit with frequent setbacks from the most evolved versions to their gruesome ancestors. Mimetic theory eventually provides an explanation for the origin of religion and a number of phenomena linked to it (from the centrality of sacrifice in every religion to the common structures of mythical narrative that can be traced in cultures as far away as Ancient Greeks and Native Polynesians).

In the most recent developments, Girard and his scholars have started to apply mimetic theory also to the explanation of historical and social processes. Far from trying to become a "theory of everything human" (that have a regrettable tendency to develop into totalitarian ideologies), mimetic theory openly declares its limits and domain of applicability. While dealing with inter-individual relationship, ("interdividual" in the theory jargon), mimetic theory clearly states that it does not provide an explanation nor a model for fundamental modes of interaction of people like love and parent-child relationship, unless for some well defined pathological forms like jealousy and the "double bind" phenomena observed for example by Gregory Bateson in the development of schizophrenia.

I report two examples where mimetic theory provides brilliant interpretations of social and historical processes, namely the existence of symbiotic ethnic groups and western modern history (or, in Haidt speech, the development of WEIRD societies). Symbiotic societies (e.g. the Parsi of India, the Mon of Thailand, and of course the Jews of the West) appear in the most disparate geographic, temporal and cultural contexts and they consist in a broader, stronger community farming out mimetically dangerous jobs like trade, medicine and banking to a minority that is tolerated in good times and can be used as scapegoat during bad ones. All the typical activities of the guest minority deal with tasks that, while essential to the whole of society, involve a greater risk of igniting rivalry and conflict because they are all centered around mediation, that can spark both positive and negative imitation. Trade is by definition based on comparisons and competition. Lawyers thrive in the resolution of conflicts. Doctors often handle extreme pain and grief situations, that especially in ancient societies tend to border with sorcery and jinx. And finally, nothing like money can spark envy and resentment and has therefore to be managed particularly carefully and "professionally".

The host majority lives within well defined boundaries, shielded by the effects of other people's envy by the system of rituals and prohibitions enforced by the main group or tribe. Indeed, enjoying the protection of a tribe means also to accept obligations like being ready to join in retaliation if some of the members have suffered any harm. When it comes to the interpretation of the birth of WEIRD societies, mimetic theory asserts in a very politically incorrect way that this stems from a radical difference between Judeo-Christian tradition and all other religions, that lies in the full revelation of the scapegoat mechanism.

Unlike all other myths, the Bible and the Gospel systematically side with the victims and this revelation peaks with the accounting of the Passion of Jesus. Whether you believe or not in Resurrection, by reading the accounts of the Passion no one can have the least doubt of who the bad guys are, or actually that everybody is a bad guy except the one that is condemned to death so that "all the others can survive". Read the Oedipus, and it is apparent that all the evils that plague the city of Thebes are to be blamed entirely on the impious Oedipus, who killed his father and married his mother, and on no one else.

By revealing the mechanism that has kept ancient communities together, Judeo-Christian tradition also opens the door to unlimited competition, escalation, and ultimately violence because scapegoating requires people to be fully unaware of its dynamics for the community to reap the benefits of the guilt transfer. The very same fact that we call somebody or something a scapegoat means that we do not really believe in it and therefore its effects in terms of containment of rivalry and conflict will be somehow limited. Western holy scripture progressively erodes the effectiveness of the system of the "sacred" that was used by mankind as a way to externalize violence.

In the Righteous Mind there is a proof point of this trend when Haidt quotes the work of Barbara Ehrenreich on how Christianity dropped dancing from its rituals, in the trajectory of the removal of the old sacred world of myth. Between

Renaissance and Reform, it was apparent that while the old gods had lost their authority after 1000 years of Christianity, this very same Christianity, torn apart in the bloodshed of the wars of religion and the rush to conquer new worlds, was also far away from being the Kingdom of God. What emerged, from a mimetic point of view, was a new model where scarcity replaced the sacred. And as much as the sacred is not an institution but rather the mould of ancient institutions, so scarcity turned out to be the mould of modern institutions.

If scapegoating does no longer work, and the sacred is progressively voided of its force, individuals progressively lose the obligations that tie them to their tribe, restricting them to close relatives. Where there used to be the risk of large public rivalries and conflicts that could extend to the whole community, there is now a multitude of private conflicts that do not spread thanks to the loosened tribal ties but these background conflicts give the evidence that it is very difficult, actually impossible to satisfy the desires and maybe even the needs of everyone.

So, by not recognizing the mimetic origin of desire modernity found universal scarcity as the sole possible explanation. We all crave for someone else's things, and we observe that in the long run (and even with increased income) the situation does not improve. If we still do not recognize the mechanism of desire, the obvious conclusion is that there are not enough resources to make us all happy.

The most efficient management of scarcity, as economic theory and the history of the West show, requires the setup of a market regulated by prices for resources to be optimally allocated, a legal system to transfer property rights of goods and a State empowered to enforce all this on a reasonably large area. Sacred and scarcity are just two different and mutually exclusive mimetic modes that people have found to deal with the unpleasant effects of mimetic desire. Sacred applies to traditional societies where violence is contained (in the sense of limited) in terms of prohibitions and rituals and it contains (in the sense of using) violence in the sacrifice of the scapegoat. Scarcity appears in WEIRD societies that reject sacrifice as mechanism of regulation and limit violence by privatizing conflicts and removing sacred ties between the vast majority of their members.

However, WEIRD societies see the appearance of replacement victims in the masses of those who lose their private battles and are progressively excluded from social and economic life by the indifference of the other players. I do not mean at all that scarcity is a purely cultural invention, as there are lots of situations where real scarcity of primary goods arises.

It is indeed interesting to contrast how traditional and modern societies react to the most typical case of scarcity, that is famine. Ritual and tribal obligations of traditional societies would mandate the better off to start sharing their reserve of food with the less fortunate, that in turn would be regulated by the very same system to kind of moderate their requests. Failure to comply with the rules would entail the risk of triggering a mimetic crisis to which the only answer of the community would be the sacrifice. As the famine worsens, mimetic crises progressively select new victims freeing up more resources for those left until the famine is over. The victim selection process might be coded in some ritual or happen on a random basis (most likely, it would start in a somehow orderly form and become increasingly random with the progressive collapse of the social order), eventually the survivors would be a set made mostly of members of the ruling class and a variety of clever, ruthless and outright lucky members of other classes. For the survivors, the victims would have been the price to pay to satisfy the wrath of the gods.

In modern society, the onset of famine sends the price of food skyrocketing, with the poor being progressively left to starvation and also some of the rich if famine continues to stress the social structure beyond the point where enforcement of mutual indifference by law can no longer be guaranteed. The final outcome of severe famine does not differ much from that of traditional societies, that is survivors would most likely be members of the ruling class plus the fittest of the lower classes. Survivors again would look back and wonder whether all had been done to minimize the number of victims. After all, two thousand years of Christianity did not pass in vain and the scandal for unjustified sacrifice and a compassion for the explicit victims have somehow engrained in the Western attitude. In both cases, the survivors would be at least relieved of their sense of guilt as the victims "deserved" to be sacrificed in traditional society or "there was nothing more we could do" for them in modern society.

In real life crises, what tends to happen is a mix of the two, with the State acting as a surrogate of the tribal system. As the two modes of social mimesis coexist in actual societies even though they are conceptually exclusive, they inevitably open the unsolvable famine debate of whether the famine was exacerbated by the avidity of grain merchants or by the incompetence of the public authority that meddled with market laws and prevented optimal resource allocation.

The move from traditional to modern society also changed the meaning of solidarity. Far from being an uncontrolled outbreak of social Darwinism, liberalism started with a deep interest for the interaction between individuals, to the extent that Adam Smith considered far more important his "Theory of moral sentiments" with respect to the much more famous "Wealth of Nations". Indeed, for Adam Smith individuals have a natural tendency to empathize and look for other people approval when it comes to moral evaluation of actions, and the experiments run by Haidt on the effects of the others' opinion in moral decisions confirm Smith's position. While solidarity in traditional societies is more of a social obligation enforced by the system of rituals and prohibitions, in modern society it is a prize that must be gained every day by means of an honorable, fair and gentle interaction with other people, and this conduct, as Benjamin Franklin noted, is also the one that makes us look reliable from a business perspective.

Even if we might be driven by the private vices described by Mandeville in his "Tale of the Bees", when it comes to action we always consider the judgment of the "man without" of Adam Smith and this shapes us in a form that helps build public virtues and increase the overall wealth of the nation. The irony in this process is that the mimetic nature of desire remains largely misunderstood, at least to the large majority of people and this happens despite that many of the bards of the modern nations, from Dante to Shakespeare and Cervantes, have instead developed a very precise and accurate theory of mimetic desire in their literary works.

The establishment of modernity on a base that still leaves hidden or misunderstood the true nature of human desire has also had detrimental effects on all the doctrines that tried to diagnose and overcome its illnesses. From a mimetic perspective, Marxism simply chose to take the world back to the era of the sacred solidarity, failing to understand that the main problem of modernity was not the wrong allocation of the means of production or excessive amount of religious opium in the air, but that simply after 2000 years of Christianity it was impossible to really believe in the value of sacrifice, even if they were carried out on a collective scale exterminating peasants and bourgeois by the millions. In other words, Marxism did not realize that not all religions were opium, and rather there was one tradition that albeit with varying degrees of success was curing people from the sacrificial hangover.

"Property is sacred" has been one of the foundation of the modern world, and Marx thought that the sacred was a relic on the way of a quick dismissal and focused his attention on the fight to overcome property. He should have done the opposite.

On the other hand, Freudism started from the intuition that it was more of an inner problem of man that needed attention before moving to change the social organization. The core finding of Freudism, the Oedipus complex, correctly identified that there were three elements in the human problem but somehow it restricted the area to sexuality and parental relations. In "Violence and the Sacred" Girard shows how Freud went so close to capturing the real nature of desire with the Oedipus and the origin of myths and rituals in "Totem and Taboos" but somehow fell prey to the Romantic belief that there is nothing between myself and my desired object. According to Freud, the child really desires his mother (albeit with his unconscious part), while for Girard rivalry with the father could be sparked by any object, provided that there are the conditions for internal mediation.

In sum, WEIRD societies have invested Market and State as the key structures to contain the dynamic of unconfined escalation. Over the course of the Modern era, State has become more totalitarian in the sense that it extended well beyond the initial scope of the "night watch state" to the oversized

27

dimension of the welfare state-society. Markets have become increasingly efficient and global, with the biggest companies able to rival with States in terms of power and influence. Both have initiated a rush to increase indefinitely their size, power, reach and relevance in individual lives and claim to represent the ultimate achievement of history. This giant escalation led ultimately to the World Wars of last century and recurring economic shocks of ever greater magnitude that four centuries after the European wars of religion left the founding structures of modernity alive but somehow delegitimized.

According to Girard we are therefore living in an ambiguous world that, while undoubtedly growing more aware and better at saving victims in increasing numbers, it counterbalances this trend with the relentless destruction of the traditional brakes to the escalation of violence and the increased power and availability of the means of destruction. It is not by chance that René Girard puts at the beginning of his last work a quote from the "Lettres provinciales" of Blaise Pascal: "All the efforts of violence cannot weaken truth, and they only make it more apparent. At the same time, all the light of truth cannot stop violence and it only irritates and exacerbates it more". So for Girard it is very likely that at the end of history mankind will be trapped in an Apocalypse, that will be entirely of its own making.

Chapter 3 – Mimetic challenges to moral foundations.

For all its similarities, mimesis and the moral foundation theory do not overlap and pose each other a set of challenges that should be further developed. In this chapter I define and briefly elaborate in three points the critique that mimesis poses to moral foundations, namely: failure to identify the scapegoat mechanism in the birth of religion, the reverse order of moral axis generation and some contradiction or inconsistency in dealing with the risk of totalitarianism in the balancing of the chimp and hive side of human nature. Let's start with the origin of religion.

Haidt basically buys the "hyperactive agent detection" explanation of the "New atheists" and then complements it with the theory of the sacred of Durkheim. Unlike in Canetti, there is

28

no in depth reflection on the role of packs, victims and sacrifice in cementing communities. The birth of the sanctity foundation is linked almost exclusively to the progressive evolution of practices adopted to avoid pathogens and prevent contagion. The basic problem here is that Haidt assumes the existence of a primitive form of rationality that enables hominids to create a set of hypothesis around how the world works and the skill to translate that into a mythical form, while this rationality actually emerges after the moral foundations have been laid down with non-rational means.

Mimetic theory reverses the perspective by placing the arbitrary sacrifice of a scapegoat randomly selected by a crowd under the push of utterly irrational rivalry as founding act of religion (and then morality and rationality). The unconscious transfert and the collective sense of liberation that follow create the first experience of "hiveness" and "order" from which rationality can start. In his research about several cosmogony myths, Girard shows that the mimetic crisis and the immolation of the victim always precede the creation of the universe.

Mimetic crises can arise not only from community rivalries but also from external events like epidemics. Let us imagine a group of primitive hominids that is being ravaged by a disease like leprosy. It is not difficult that in the unrest that follows victims are more likely to be selected among those most severely affected by the illness and when the selective killing of the sick leads to both social peace and eradication of the contagion the moral foundations of sanctity can eventually be set. We do not want to mean here that cause-effect reasoning played no role in helping humans develop defenses against pathogens but rather that sacrifice precedes moral reasoning in establishing the "sanctity foundation". Only after a long chain of random (but evolutionary favorable) sacrifices the ritual and "morally rational" coding follow and establish the sanctity foundation. As a last step eventually the whole experience is synthesized in the narrative of the myth for the next generations to follow on the same tracks.

Finally, the recognition of the hive side as a distinctive and positive feature of mankind puts Jon Haidt in an uncomfortable position when it comes to self-transcendence. He is the first to recognize by quoting texts from Benito Mussolini, the founder of Fascism, that the hive side can be manipulated by rogue governments to steer crowds for their totalitarian goals. This is clearly bad, but nonetheless also WEIRD governments need this type of events to satisfy this side of the human nature. In WEIRD societies you get the World Cup, the Super Bowl and down to smaller community events that are essential to generate self-transcendence (in the case of Haidt, the University of Virginia day).

So whether a crowd experience is good or bad, is morally justified or not, depends on the ultimate goals of those that organize it. As Haidt shows, these parochial communities might have moral matrices that are in complete contrast. But as they all cater to the hive side that is common to all people, these types of event are somehow all legitimate, regardless if we are talking about the Hitler rallies in Nuremberg or the Martin Luther King address in Washington.

The other point is about the relationship between knowledge and happiness. Let's assume we all get a PhD in moral foundations and mimesis and perfectly understand the hive and crowd mechanisms. Would it still be possible for us to fully cheer and enjoy a rave party or a Champions League final? Or would we risk losing out on the experience because we are aware of the underlying dynamics (and, to some extent, delusion?). My personal view is that awareness initially brings some watering down of the hive experience but somehow we have to resist the temptation of reviving it with artificial means (i.e. by damping consciousness with increasing amounts of alcohol and drugs).

I believe the solution is rather to look for newer and better hive experiences and I bring just a small exhibit to explain the concept. Back in June 2007, I was attending the yearly corporate convention, with the occasional top management speeches and the surrounding set of amenities (music, games, cocktails) meant to create a single group experience out of hundreds of individuals coming from tens of different countries. It was apparent it was not working at all, with people loitering around with half empty glasses doing some small talk with colleagues but really waiting for the time to go to bed. Then, back in my hotel room, I logged on to the Internet and connected to the streaming of the Apple convention where Steve Jobs was introducing the iPhone for the first time.

Even from the computer screen, it was apparent that the entire convention center was a single entity waiting for his every word and gesture and this was so powerful that it literally stretched out of the screen. True, Steve Jobs was always a formidable keynote presenter, but this would not explain it all. It was clear that he was literally condensing the attention and the thought of the audience because he was showing a new world, albeit a technological one. The day after at breakfast, it turned out that several of us had watched the event in the privacy of their rooms. And the impression was so powerful that even hours after the event this created an immediate solidarity among the "lonely night watchers". In short, we don't have to be afraid of knowledge spoiling our old hive experiences. We have to be afraid of the lack of visionaries, prophets, and leaders able to ignite new dreams and set new challenges.

Chapter 4 – Reverse challenges to mimesis.

Moral foundation theory far outdoes mimesis in providing experimental evidence for its findings. Assuming desire in the mimetic sense exists, can we devise an experiment where we can actually measure it or at least a proxy quantity or we have to rely solely on the ample (e.g. literary, historical, cultural and anthropological) but mostly non-clinical sources used by mimesis scholars?

By remaining a non-measurable entity, desire risks becoming yet another Freudian Unconscious, maybe a very useful concept and interpretation tool but not exactly a fully recognized scientific entity like hearts and brains. We can only sketch here a possible experiment, starting from the discovery of mirror neurons that is mentioned in both theories as key exhibit. If we follow mimesis definition, the experiments to identify the physiological traces of desire require the presence of the subject, the desired object and the mediator.

The conditions of the experiments have to be designed in a way to avoid interference with need or instinct, so for example it would not make sense to try to spot mimetic desire activity by showing a glass of water to a thirsty subject. For the very same reason, the instruments used to track human activity should be as little invasive as possible. Starting from the simplest example of the children converging on the same toy, one could start by placing a neutral object together with the subject and let the subject reach a stage where we are sure the object is of no interest to her. Yet the object needs not to be completely plain, like for example the magazines you find in waiting rooms and leave the possibility open for creative or at least unexpected behavior. At the same time, a provocative object like for example a gun would attract too much attention right from the beginning and would make spotting the effect of the mediator difficult. After the subject has got used to the object, the mediator is introduced in the environment. The mediator would focus on the object and let the subject believe she has found some unthinkable use of great satisfaction. If mimesis is correct, it should be possible to track now in the subject a new activity, possibly not even related to the one registered in the initial subject-object interaction.

The experiment should also try to reproduce the external and internal mediation, and track if, how and when the mental activity the subject diverge (internal mediations tend to end up in conflict). We do not know if today clinical instruments allow such experiments to be conceived and carried out, but for sure experimental and developmental psychology seems better equipped at building the cases than mimesis scholars.

Another point where moral foundations theory seems to have an edge or at least more attention with respect to mimesis is the role of care and love. One of the exhibits used by Haidt as proof points of the "inner lawyer" thesis is a personal experience where he found himself lying to his wife about house chores and he openly quotes feedback received from other researchers not to overlook the role of care for children with respect to the more apparent clash dynamics in the building of ancient groups. And yet, no experience of transcendence is more common to people like falling in love, and from the lover perspective this is a real, conscious transcendence originated by the loved one and not a "self-built" experience like awe for nature or some kind of tribal ritual. Mimesis also underlines the need of some kind of personal conversion to grasp its full meaning and recognize the log in our eye before the straw in the eyes of the others, but somehow remains more rooted in the realm of human rivalry and conflict.

It is maybe not a coincidence that in his master essays about the theatre of Shakespeare René Girard gives a lot of space to tragedies and comedies but little if no attention to "Romeo and Juliet". For all its apologetic intent, mimesis seems too much focused on violence and somehow overlooks the words of the book of Wisdom 1,13 ("For God did not make Death, he takes no pleasure in destroying the living. To exist -- for this he created all things; the creatures of the world have health in them, in them is no fatal poison, and Hades has no power over the world"). In a simpler way, while mimesis understands a lot about the dark side of mankind, it stops somehow short in considering the broader drive to life, pleasure, fulfillment and ultimately the rejection of death that is as much a constituent part of our soul as our tendency to fight and compete.

Chapter 5 – What if they are right?

Jonathan Haidt begins his book with the goal of helping to improve the overly factious and destructive debate now reigning in American politics between conservatives, liberals and libertarians, who champion the idea that individual desires of any kind should not be restrained by any sort of legal, moral, religious or societal bind as long as no damage is incurred by other people or, by extension, the environment. It is the case for example of same-sex marriages, all claims around biomedical research, and also absolute economic freedom like the right of each people to print her own currency.

Jon Haidt shows that all these clashes intersect and interact adding to the confusion as they refer to incompatible resolution frameworks where conflicting parties can borrow from each other ideas and other means to prevail but cannot really find a common ground for negotiation. This is also the case of fundamentalist terrorism that uses the latest technology to pursue its attacks or conversely modern democracies recurring to selective killings without any form of trial and justifying this on purely sacrificial grounds.

Despite the challenges, both moral foundation and mimetic theory share the big merit of shedding new light on the nature of conflict in general and political and moral conflict in particular. They both provide insights as to when conflict can be managed under a shared framework of values between parties or on the contrary it arises from value systems that have little or nothing in common and make conflict unsolvable by nature. Starting from this observation, the two theories strive to find a new common ground where radical conflict could be reconciled or at least they try to provide some interpretation tools to help us chart a way out of the deadlock. In the first chapter I have illustrated the concepts of moral foundations in defining and dealing with different and incompatible moral matrices, let me spend now a few words on summarizing the insights of Mimetic theory. By explaining both ancient, sacrificial conflicts and the conflicts of the new post-modern world ("scarcity" conflicts) Mimetic theory challenges both main flavors of the current political thought, that is liberalism and socialism.

As far as socialism is concerned, Mimetic theory reverses the optimism of Hegel, and shows that there is no end to human competition as this will continue to the end of mankind. At the same time, it demonstrates that the State is yet another superstition that must be deconstructed in the path to the end of history (which, at least according to Girard, has a high chance of ending up in apocalyptic self-destruction). And yet, no being is as social as man, as people move forward only through imitation and cannot escape the "wisdom of crowds".

Liberalism, on the other hand, can embrace the vision of man as a competitive being, and might somehow concede that competition poses risks that have to be managed by a lean state focused on the prevention of violence and conflict. However, it can hardly accept that there is basically no such thing as an "independent rational individual", as two individuals would immediately start imitating each other desires, or their most intimate essence.

Mimetic theory can be interpreted both in a transcendentalist and materialist way, and this can help bridging the gap in the ever increasing conflict between religious and radically non-religious thought. René Girard opted for the transcendentalist approach, and converted to Christianity while studying mimetic desire. Girard has been openly declaring throughout his career that, while using a rigorously scientific method, one could see mimetic theory as an "anthropological apology" of Christianity in general and Roman Catholicism in particular.

This has drawn to him at once the hostility of non-religious scholars that considered him a theologian in disguise and also the one of full-service theologians that considered his theory as a Gnostic attempt to scientifically explain faith and religion. As Girard points out, given the self-referential and hidden nature of the scapegoat mechanism, only a Revelation from God can set man free from its trap.

But mankind has repeatedly rejected to fully embrace Christianity, in all its ancient, Middle Age and modern varieties, so the result is that we are at the mercy of unleashed mimetic rivalry that will ultimately wipe away all the structures elaborated over time to restrain it. We see that State and Market, the two structures emerged in modernity to replace the mythological structures eroded by Christianity are increasingly losing legitimacy and hence restraining power. We do not know if a new restraining structure will emerge, if not the time of Lawlessness is close to arrive.

This might not be such a bad thing, according to a non-religious or outright atheist interpretation of mimetic theory. If we assume that mankind is based on mimetic desire and we are alone on this rock in the middle of the universe, it was only a question of time and statistical probability for one of the tribes that appeared on the planet to start getting the right reading of the scapegoat mechanism. First, the scapegoat mechanism would defend early human communities against self-destruction.

Then, over time and with a bit of luck, one of these communities would eventually get the right interpretation and take humanity to the next step. By pure chance, this tribe happened to be the Jews, and the Jew that came out with the perfect interpretation was so successful to be rejected by his own people, proof that indeed a step change in understanding had taken place. From this point of view, the trajectory is set and "Lawlessness" is indeed the final paradise. Like in the Hegelian perspective, we know what man will look like in the end of time, and we know that the process is painful. Unlike in Marx and

Hegel, we have objectively less reasons to be optimistic that mankind will eventually get to that point or rather get the situation irremediably out of control in the middle journey for having removed the brakes too early or too abruptly.

There is no scientific or rational way to judge which one of the two interpretations is true, choosing between the two is indeed a decision grounded in freedom, just like deciding to convert to a faith or not. Finally, if mimetic and moral foundations theory can help establish a new cultural framework, what practical means can be adopted to help contain the multiple conflicts between individuals, individuals and society and at the largest scale the states themselves?

For individuals (both considered as singles and as "parochial" groups with similar core interests and aspirations) the beginning of an answer could be in the broad notion of "accessible desire". Desire can be restrained or at least managed if there are places where it can be satisfied and this place is in principle accessible to interested parties.

Conservative societies see the appearance of neighborhoods or even whole cities and states devoted to gaming, drugs but also plastic surgery and artificial insemination. And conversely, liberal societies have to come to terms with groups that decide to commit themselves to non-liberal lifestyles, like the Amish in the United States or the growing conservative Muslim communities in Europe. The main problem with this approach is that to be truly effective it should somehow guarantee an opt-out/opt-in right to the individual, and that would often imply freedom of immigration between sovereign entities that are, to say the least, unwilling to grant this right.

However, modern conflicts since the end of World War 2 have implied the ever increasing growth of the number of refugees and immigration has become a global trend that affects all societies. If modernity has been defined by the mutual recognition of ethnic and geographic entities that shared a common belief in the sovereign state and the market economy and regulated the flow of trade and war while keeping people static in their respective cultural tradition, post modernity could be defined also by the mutual recognition of spiritual entities (in terms of homogeneous direction of desires), somehow tied but not necessarily identified with a geographic and sovereign entity that regulate the flow of people that choose to identify with them while keeping their ideal blueprint unchanged (or at least evolving with its own dynamics).

This would obviously not prevent conflicts from erupting, and they would most likely be of the worst species, the unsolvable one. With a bit more optimistic view than the one of Girard and Pascal, I believe that a growing comprehension of the dynamics of desire and sacrifice in political leadership and the general public can help restrain the rush to unsolvable conflicts (otherwise I would not be writing these booklets).

Some good examples of leadership aware of the sense of self-sacrifice can be found in "Too Big to Fail", the insider account of the months that led to the demise of Lehman Brothers in September 2008, the near collapse of the global financial system and its rescue by the TARP program adopted in a hurry by the US Government. The story of the financial crisis is indeed full of mimetic behaviors and feelings (e.g. resentment, reputation, contagion, panic keep recurring throughout the book) along with examples of scapegoating. I would just recall the voluntary humiliation that then Secretary of Treasury and former Wall Street titan Henry Paulson self-inflicted himself by kneeling in front of Democrat House Speaker Nancy Pelosi to save the TARP deal and probably the world economy in the middle of Congressional panic. A public educated in the dynamics of mimesis and moral foundations could be in a position to appreciate the providential step back and the turning of the other cheek that up to now in real world politics has been tantamount to failure.

Bibliography

"Crowds and Power" by Elias Canetti

"The Righteous Mind" by Jonathan Haidt

"Violence and the Sacred" by René Girard

"Things hidden from the foundation of the world" by René Girard

"Desire, deceit and the novel" by René Girard

"Desire and the West: Market, State and the Containment of Armageddon" by Luca Luchesini

"Too Big to Fail" by Andrew Ross Sorkin

Power, Crowds, Violence and Desire in E.Canetti and R.Girard

Introduction

This essay has a twofold aim: the first is to nail down the key ideas about the origin of power and the behavior of human crowds as explained by Elias Canetti in his monumental work "Crowds and Power" that won him the Nobel Prize for Literature in 1981. The second is to try to connect the dots between the thought of Canetti and the one of another great literate and anthropologist of the 20th century, René Girard who also investigated the behavior of crowds from the perspective of the birth of myths and religion.

I believe and try to prove that Canetti actually complements Girard findings so that the two must be adopted to account for the complex dynamics and interconnections between power, violence and religion, both in the early stages of human development and in the following evolution of history.

The book is structured as follows: Chapter 1 provides some biographical background about Elias Canetti. Chapter 2 summarizes the theory of crowds and Chapter 3 instead introduces the subject of power. In Chapter 4 I will try to clarify the connection between the two concepts, while Chapter 5 puts Canetti in relationship with Girard research about mimetic desire, crowds and the scapegoat mechanism. Finally, Chapter 6 sketches some lines of further reflection about the meaning of political action at large after the illuminating and desacralizing critique that these two thinkers have carried out around some of the core categories that every human being experiences in her life.

Chapter 1 – The life of Elias Canetti

Elias Canetti (1905-1994) was born in Rustchuck (nowadays Ruse), in the then Ottoman-ruled Bulgaria from a Spanish Jew family. His parents then decided to move to England, where his father prematurely died from a stroke in 1912. Elias and his two younger brothers were then brought up by their mother and spent their youth between Vienna, Zurich and

Frankfurt until 1938 when Elias and his family fled to London to escape the Austrian annexation to Nazi Germany. After the end of the war, Canetti obtained the British citizenship and eventually moved back to his beloved Switzerland in 1988 to spend the last years of his life.

In his autobiographical novel "The Tongue Set Free" Canetti vividly recalls one of his first experiences of dealing with crowds: just arrived in Vienna from England in 1914 at the onslaught of World War 1, the three small Canetti children had the unfortunate idea of singing the British anthem "God save the King" in the middle of the Prater park and were quickly sorrounded by a scolding crowd of bystanders that restrained from physical aggression only thanks to the age of the singers.

The interest of Canetti into the essence and behavior of crowds resurfaced during his teenage years spent in Frankfurt in the early 1920s, when he witnessed and lived the social upheavals created by the German hyperinflation and eventually he personally took part to the mass demonstrations that stormed and set on fire the Courts of Vienna on July 15th 1927. Since that moment, even though he graduated in Chemistry and started his career as a novelist his main interest became to investigate and clarify the way crowds behave and their intimate essence. Canetti would present his findings in "Crowds and Power", a work that appeared in 1960, 33 years after the blaze in Vienna.

However, Canetti himself never considered this work exhaustive and still in 1980 he openly wrote that the essence of crowds and its associated phenomena was still elusive to his attempts of understanding.

Chapter 2 – Crowds

Canetti starts his treaty on crowds and power by observing the psychological experience that leads people to join a crowd and the various types of crowd that can ensue. Early in his youth years Canetti had an almost mystical experience where he realized that the drive to form a crowd is a basic pulsion of the human being and at the same time he rejected the findings of contemporary psychoanalysis (he was one of the first readers of "Introduction to the psychology of masses" of Sigmund Freud) on the grounds that it was failing to put this as a founding concept just like the Oedipus. Why do people have a compelling pulse to join crowds?

Because they provide an antidote, albeit temporary, to the typical human trend of differentiation and take people back to a state where they are equal to each other and without any bound. Let's elaborate more on this. People tend inexorably to differentiate, from any point of view, from the social structure which progressively defines the role, responsibility and position of each individual within political and professional hierarchies, to the knowledge development process whereby each one of us keeps shaping a certain competence in a well-defined field to the sentimental one where we evolve from the original indifferentiation of the newborn with respect to the her mother to the development of one's own and unique network of family and friendship relations.

We are not trying to determine here whether this process is linear or with traumatic discontinuities, nor intended or random (it shows indeed all of these features). We simply state that differentiation is always at work, whatever its causes or ways. And yet, as much as this process is crucial in shaping our own individuality it is at the same time the first constraint to our desire of infinite freedom and immortality, in short human desire as such (I have to warn the reader that, unlike Girard, Canetti does not identify desire explicitly in his work).

By removing any external distinction (all members of a crowd are the same regardless of their individuality) and providing the instant experience of being part of a much bigger whole, (crowds are measured by the thousands of elements at least) crowds fulfill, albeit temporarily, this basic desire of mankind. The moment in which a group of people dumps individuality and becomes behaving as a single entity in a crowd is called the discharge. It can be induced with some specific techniques like e.g. singing, marching or even the attack of an external force like anti-riot police. From this moment on, the crowd behaves and reacts as one single being. In this state, the crowd can also flee a specific threat, however it is very different from panic. In the panic state, people have gained back control of their individuality and start seeing all the other members of the crowd as an obstacle. The resulting confusion is rather the consequence of the loss of the crowd state (the so-called eruption) than its true manifestation.

Crowds can indeed flee, reorganize and react orderly to every attack as long as their members retain the "discharged" attitude. However, at some point in time crowds erupt naturally and every individual returns to its previous position in life and society (if, of course, in the meantime the action of the crowd has not led to major changes in the old order).

Canetti classifies crowds based on their dominant sentimental attitude and their spatial collocation: crowds can be baited against a specific enemy or class of enemies, or they can be unified by the movement toward a common goal (either real or ideal) or away from a common threat. Most often, crowds find balance when they can confront another opposing crowd (the double crowd concept) whereby the two entities, while trying to overrule each other, provide also the primary reason of being to each other. Double crowds typically apply to national and party rivalries, but also extend to the basic symbolic notions of the living and the dead or males and females. The parliamentary system eventually sublimates this dynamic by fixing the two opposing crowds of the majority and the opposition and their clash in the vote mechanism.

Moving to the symbolic plane, Canetti shows that the first basic elements that mankind had to master in its evolution like fire, the water of seas, rivers and rain, the trees of the forests, the sands of the deserts or the herds of wild animals all had to some extent the distinct charcteristic of crowds: they are made by many smaller elements, they can behave as a unity and spread in an unstoppable way incorporating everything they find on their way. Canetti does not explain in detail how the experience of these phenomena of natural crowds influenced the primitive man, however when it comes to the genesis of the crowd, Canetti observes that to start a crowd it is necessary to have a smaller group of people that can identify themselves with the goal of the future crowd and act as a catalyzer for the bigger crowd to form, if the right environmental conditions arise.

This catalyzer is the crowd crystal and is indeed the first structure that for Canetti appeared in the history of mankind in the form of the pack of primitive societies. By applying the same taxonomic approach used for the crowd to its ancestor, the pack, Canetti identifies four types of pack: the hunting pack, the war pack, the lamenting pack and the increase pack. These packs can mutually transform into each other.

The hunting pack and its hierarchy are shared with similar structures of the animal world. It is only with mankind however that the war, increase and lamenting pack appear for the first time. What is the difference between hunting and war packs? While hunting packs are directed at animals and driven mainly by the need to procure food, war packs are directed exclusively at other rival human groups and can be triggered also by futile grounds of provocation. Hegel would say that these are the first distinctive human actions.

The hierarchy tasks evolve as well: the leader of human packs must manage very precisely the booty allocation between the members of the pack. Unlike in animals where after the hunt hierarchy translates simply in the respect of a fixed pecking order, hierachies in people are always at risk of being challenged by the relentless action of desire and envy. The booty obtained in hunt and war helps also transform the war pack into an increase pack, that is to say a group of people defined by some kind of ritual whose goal is the increase of the amount of cattle, food, slaves or any other good needed by the community or conquered in a successful campaign. No matter how successful, some members of the community perished in action, and then the lamenting pack fulfills the double goal of at once re-asserting the unity of the survivors in their grief for the dead and establishing the mirror crowd of the dead to whom the perished members of the community are handed over. Of course, a pack lamenting the dead in battle can turn into a war pack and so on. Canetti also sees the birth of the lamenting pack as a way to discharge the psychological strain that the pain of the victims of the war/hunting pack creates, a kind of purification ritual for the winners. The lamenting pack is also the ground upon which every religion is built, and Canetti provides many examples of rituals that have arrived to this day in Christian and Islamic rituals.

Concluding the part of his treatise on crowds, Canetti touches on two very modern aspects, inflation and the symbols of crowds of modern European nations. Inflation, besides being an economic headache, is for Canetti an even worse plague as it attacks directly the value of the crowd itself, which, we remind, is with individuality one of the two "core pulsions" that make people live. The first attack of inflation is the classic devaluation of assets, like e.g. bank accounts denominated in a certain currency. Beyond practical implications, the value of everyone's personal treasury is also linked to its continuous increase over lifetime, which is real as long as inflation is kept under control. Excessive inflation nixes the possibility of increasing one's personal treasury, which is also a crowd symbol. Secondly, and even worse on an ontological plane, inflation to some extent also devalues numbers. If a million Reichsmark is all of a sudden worth nothing, this applies both to the Reichsmark and to the million. But the million is also the unity used to measure crowds of other things, including people. Inflation causes at once the devaluation of things and the devaluations of groups of people and eventually of entire nations, which can eventually feel under attack and start searching for an enemy. According to Canetti, this is precisely the dyanmics that Hitler exploited to gain power and bait the Germans against the Jews.

The last comments on crowds are a reflection about the symbols of crowds that act as a common reference to the different European nations and that pre-exist to any conscious explanation of the common historical and cultural links between their members. The British have as symbol of crowd the sea, or more precisely the commander of a ship at sea that has to chart its route across the dangers of the immense ocean and thereby dominate this immensity. Germans before the wars had the army as unifying symbol, and the army was personified by their forests, with soldiers being the individual trees. It is not a chance that the highest German military decorations had oak leaves, and it is maybe not a chance either that in post-World War 2 Germany was the country where the environmentalist movement in the 1970s became a political movement to defend forests against acid rains. Modern France has its symbol in the crowds of the Revolution, Switzerland in its mountains and the Netherlands in the dikes that protect it from the North Sea. It is interesting that up to the 1960 when he wrote the book Canetti was not able to find a distinct symbol of crowd for Italy as the attempt of Fascism to revive ancient Roman symbols had failed nor could modern Italy use the crowds assembled in St.Peter Square as they served the more universal purposes of the Roman Catholic Church. In retrospect and after two victories in the World Cup in post-war times, I would say that the symbol of crowds Italians have engrained in their identity now is the one of the football stadium.

Chapter 3 – Power

While Canetti uses for the explanation of crowds an almost mathematical approach with definitions, logical deductions and proof points, he begins the description of power from a very different perspective, by analyzing the core mechanism of food processing and its associated organs, namely the hands and their extensions to grab the prey, the mouth to kill and crush it and the stomach and other hidden digestive organs to assimilate it.

In other words, the variety of forms that power has taken in human history with all its associated institutions, symbols and rituals ultimately rely on the core violence of the predator-pray relationship. Canetti identifies three core aspects of power: the Survivor who rules via Commands and establishes links between living things with Transformations or metamorphosis. We have demonstrated in the previous chapter that the predator-prey relationship is experienced by people in the various forms of the hunting and warring packs that give birth to the figure of the Survivor.

In a way similar to the Master of the Hegelian dialectic, the Survivor is the one that came back alive and victorious from the hunt or the war, thereby establishing its power not only on the dead enemies but also on the dead friends. The more the dead in the battle, the more power is granted to the Survivor and the more his community is guaranteed to benefit from his leadership in increasing its rule among the neighboring communities. It is the Survivor who oversees how to split the prey or the loot among the different members of the pack: it is up to him to define who gets what, always following a very precise and intricate ritual that mimics the one used by the religious leader in managing the religious sacrifice (the two roles are often interchangeable). The three key principles set by Carl Schmitt at the origin of right, that is the seizure of the territory ("Nehmen"), its allocation to the members of the community ("Teilen") and its exploitation to increase the overall welfare of the community ("Weiden") find here their primeval ancestor in the hunting and war packs led by the survivors of earlier fights.

However, the paradox that arises is devilish: to cement his power, the Survivor needs to increase the crowd of the dead, and while the primary and explicit targets are indeed the enemies of the opposing crowds, there will be more and more casualties also among his own community. The harsh reality is that the Survivor power benefits from both types of death while the community at some point in time will see the cost-benefit balance enter into a crisis mode that can find a solution only in the self-destruction of the community or in the ousting of the ruler.

When it comes to command, Canetti makes the crucial observation that command precedes language and is founded in the pre-human and cross-species interaction of the flight command, to which any pray obeys as soon as the presence or even the suspect of presence of the predator is detected. Canetti traces all subsequent evolutions of command to the threat of death by devouration. Even when animals obey, for instance, to trainers in an action-reward scheme, they do so under the threat of some kind of physical punishment. So command, far from being a human peculiarity, is indeed rooted in nature and precedes language and every other symbolic structure.

What is mankind adding to this basic interaction? In people, every command creates a feedback sting in those that receive it, a resentment to retaliate and transfer the very same command to someone else at a later date. It does not really matter how and when the transfer happens, neither if the transfer affects the subject that gave the initial command. The key point is to have the possibility to offload this reminder that eventually relies on a threat of punishment and a more or less explicit reminder of death. How to cure it? It is either the promise of a promotion (transform from slave and potential victim/pray to master and predator) or the discharge in a reversal crowd at the expense of the Survivor or the ruling class.

The third element introduced by power in the horizon of mankind is transformation and it begins right during the hunt, where hunters feel the pray or mimic its sounds, smell and sights to better attract it into a trap. Preys and especially enemies enact every type of transformation to flee (by becoming fish to escape via swimming through a river, or running like horses). And rulers learn to hide and conceal their true intention while at the same time simulating and impersonating different ones to defend and extend their power over the community. At the same time, rulers cannot help transforming space around them with cities, buildings, triumph arches and the like to mark their existence.

Chapter 4 – Relationship between Crowds and Power

The connection between crowds and power is now clear. Deeply rooted in the violent origins of mankind, hunting and war packs lead to the emergence of the Survivor, who fulfills a triple role: he guarantees peaceful pray repartition, he ensures the increase of resources for the community and he is granted absolute power over the members of the community to eradicate with his arbitration any risk of disorder due to internal conflicts. Power needs crowds to assert itself and as object of its commands and this is counterbalanced by the fact that the crowd mght rebel and become a toppling crowd where the rulers become the designated victims. This is leading to the paranoia of the powerful people, who typically see themselves surrounded by hostile crowds (be them people, animals, spirits, eyes, they are always persecuted by crowds).

But crowds need power to keep them together and extend through the physical presence of their leaders the feeling of unity and harmony first perceived in the victorious battle. To this extent, crowds are willing to confer to their rulers the right of death over their members as foundation of command. The power of the king can continue as long as the increase of the community from pack to crowd is granted, but increasing the well-being of the community implies a growing level of command that slowly builds up sting mass in that very same crowd until reversal crowds do away more or less violently with the existing order and build a new one. Power cannot help continuously seeding the roots of its own destruction, often a violent one.

Chapter 5 – Canetti in a Girardian perspective

There are striking similarities in the methods of Canetti and Girard: both recur freely to disparate sources and tools, from anthropology reports describing the primitive tribes survived to our days to the literary analysis of myths and finally to the analysis of psychological disturbances (schizophrenia in the case of Girard and paranoia in the case of Canetti).

Both try to pin down the key mechanisms of hominization taking as much as possible into account the experience of the early men in an evolutionary perspective and trying to derive the hominization processes from pre-existing structures present also in the animal world. While Girard focuses on the intra-community aspects of rivalry that eventually lead to the scapegoating mechanism, Canetti turns his attention to the inter-community aspects that are essentially ruled by warfare and hunting and that ground the basic notion of pack.

Both agree in recognizing violence and the way it is managed by the primitive community as a key driver of human evolution, and both would eventually agree with Hegel in setting desire (of someone else's desire in the case of Girard or in an unlimited desire of self-assertion at the expense of others in the case of Canetti) as the key factor of anthropogenesis, albeit with very different perspectives on the final outcome. René Girard openly acknowledges the value of the work of Canetti in his fundamental work "Violence and the Sacred" while it is not clear, at least to me, if Canetti was aware of Girard anthropological findings.

And yet, somehow both fail to recognize each other findings. Canetti remains almost completely blind to the scapegoating mechanism, even though he gives an almost perfect description of it in "Crowds and Power" and has been exposed to vivid examples of it in his youth.

One of Canetti best friends, Thomas Marek, was a brilliant student of philosophy that had been crippled by complete body paralysis and spent his time studying on a wheelchair attended by his mother. The two met in 1930 and soon Canetti started to share his reflections about crowds and the way people actually try to become part of a crowd to feel the experience of complete equality. To his surprise, Thomas did not share the point of view, as most of the time he had experienced crowds he had played what in mimetic theory is the part of the scapegoat.

To prove this, Marek recalled the meetings of the Vienna invalid association where he was regularly attending and where he was the odd one out, as he was clearly much more crippled than all the others ("These people after all only lacked an arm or a leg or an eye") and at the same time far superior intellectually ("I could not bear with attending yet another trade union where members were reading only "The Crippleds' Gazette"). The picture for Thomas Marek is very clear: "I had the very distinct impression that all these people were *envying* me". He continues: "My mother pulled me out of the room, but I would have remained to see if they would finally attack me". Canetti recalls this experience in 1980, after another 20 years of reflection after the appearance of "Crowds and Power" and yet is not able to name explicitly the reverse mechanism of the "survivor".

On the other hand, in the reflection of Girard power is just a consequence of the deferral of the sacrificing of the victim, which is granted unlimited power over the community until the time of her sacrifice comes. Not surprisingly, both Girard and Canetti pay a lot of attention to the sacred monarchies of Africa, where the King is at once supreme ruler and designated scapegoat. Canetti somehow unveils a reverse scapegoating mechanism where actually either the victim is able to physically win over the crowd (the survivor) or the crowd itself recognizes the winner due to some extrenal cause (e.g. a successful fight etc.) without triggering a mimetic rivalry that would undermine his authority.

Chapter 6 – Toward a new political philosophy?

Canetti and Girard helped unveil the lies or at least the delusions or misrepresentations at the heart of the two core categories of Power and Religion (as you cannot have any true society without any of these) but now that we have realized this on what truth will we ground our development?

As Andre Malraux said, we have unveiled all the lies but we still do not know what the truth is. Let's summarize first the key findings of the research of Canetti and Girard. The core driver of man, or its essence, is the presence of desire, that is a pulsion without any specific object (unlike needs or instincts which do have a specific object that satisfies them) that pushes man to look for recognition of its existence.

This was originally highlighted by Hegel and refined by the following thinkers, and Girard complemented it with the discovery that desire is actually mimetic, that is lacking a specific object of satisfaction desire imitates other desires, that is we tend to long for the things that other people want just because they want them. This lays at once the foundations for positive and negative imitation that leads to the unmatched creativity of mankind and its perennial potential for destructive conflict. To avoid self-destruction, we need a mechanism to limit the violence that can burst at any time. Canetti and Girard here identify two ways by which order and structure can appear out of conflict and violence: the survivor-pack dynamic that takes place mostly in the relationship of a human community with the outside world and the scapegoating mechanism that can be triggered when intra-community conflicts disrupt the social order. To be effective, both mechanisms require the unawareness or misrepresentation of the members of crowd: the scapegoating crowd must be persuaded in good faith that the designated victim is the one and only responsible of all the evil that is unsettling the community.

The commanded crowd instead must believe that its ruler is devoted to the continuous defense and increase of some measure of its essence, be it food, number of its members, their spiritual well being and so on, while instead there is an irresolvable conflict of interest between rulers and crowds. Canetti and Girard then move on to show how these misrepresentations can ground the foundations of respectively the State and ancient myth and religion and how all of this actually helped build mankind as we know it over the last 15.000 years.

Assuming that Canetti and Girard are right in highlighting how the foundations of Power and Religion (or, in other words, of order and meaning in personal and social life) can be traced back to a boiling pot of sheer violence and unlimited desire of self-assertion, on what grounds can we ask people to abide by government laws and refrain from unleashing their desires?

And conversely, if the very essence of people is to follow the desire of being and recognition that risks pitting them one against the other, how can the state prevent or manage conflicts without at the same time jeopardizing the creativity that undeniably arises from this dynamic? Can the State still claim any role in the discipline of public and private behaviours when its origins and the order it establishes have been traced back to an arbitrary act of violence? But if we deprive the state and politics of any moral relevance and reduce them to mere keepers of the order or limiters of violent behavior, what common reference can be established between the members of such society other than the counting of votes and guarantees of mutual non-interference between groups of people following radically different beliefs?

If we classify for the sake of simplicity the current political thought lines along the very broad denominations of liberalism and socialism, we see that neither of them can fully manage the challenge.

The problem that Canetti and Girard pose to socialism is that they actually reverse the optimism of Hegel, and show that there is no end to human competition as this will continue to the end of mankind. At the same time, they show that the State is yet another superstition that must be deconstructed in the path to the end of history (which, at least according to Girard, has a high chance of ending up in apocalyptic self-destruction). And yet, no being is as social as man, as people move forward only through imitation and cannot escape the "crowd call".

Liberalism, on the other hand, can embrace the vision of man as a competitive being, and might somehow concede that competition poses risks that have to be managed by a lean state focused on the prevention of violence and conflict. However, it can hardly accept that there basically is no such thing as an "independent individual" as two individual would immediately start imitating each other desire, or their most intimate essence.

Bibliography

"Crowds and Power" by Elias Canetti (It. ed. Adelphi 1996)

"The Torch in my Ear" by Elias Canetti (It. ed. Adelphi 2005)

"The Tongue Set Free" by Elias Canetti (It.ed. Adelphi 2002)

"The nomos of the Earth" by Carl Schmitt (It.ed. Adelphi 2003)

"Violence and the Sacred" by René Girard (It.ed. Adelphi 1992)

Desire and the West: Market, State and the Containment of Armageddon

Introduction

What has given the West its supremacy over other civilizations in the last few centuries of the modern era? And why despite its undeniable success the modern way of living and thinking is still not completely accepted by a large part of the world, including all those civilizations that are trying to benefit from its most successful institutions like the free market and the sovereign state? Do Jews have any special role in the development of modernity? Why have they been blamed with the shortcomings of the modern world and yet have become one of their greatest victims? If the history of the West is also the history of the progressive secularization of society, on what grounds can be built a society that has demystified all sacred foundations?

This essay tries connecting the dots between three works that shed a new light on the peculiarity of Western civilization, using the mimetic theory of René Girard as main interpretation tool. The first one is "Civilization. West and the Rest" by Niall Ferguson, where the Harvard historian tries to identify what he calls the "killer applications" that made the political and economic rise of the West unstoppable in the Modern era (from ca. 1500 to present day).

The second one is "The Jewish Century" by Yuri Slezkine, a professor of history at Berkeley that focuses on the role of the Jews in the development of Eastern European society in the late 1800 and early 1900 and their prominent role both in the Soviet Revolution and in the rise of American Capitalism.

Finally, the third one is an essay by Massimo Cacciari, an Italian philosopher and politician that provides a new interpretation to the "katechon" concept expressed by Saint Paul in his second epistle to the Thessalonians. The three works address very different aspects of the Western civilization, ranging from political theology to economic and social analysis. Yet I try to demonstrate that all three can be derived from a common interpretation framework grounded on the principles of mimetic theory developed by René Girard and his school.

According to mimetic theory, the main differentiator of Western civilization with respect to the others lies in the revelation of the scapegoat mechanism enabled by the Judeo-Christian tradition that progressively lifts all ritual and mythical barriers and unleashes human desire that due to its mimetic and triangular nature cannot but spark emulation and competition between people. In this process, Market and State are the modern structures developed to contain desire, where containing means at once being in a position to limit its excesses but also having desire as part of one own nature.

The book is structured as follows: Chapter 1 starts with the exposition of the findings of Niall Ferguson. Chapter 2 connects them to the role of the Jews in modernity as explained by Yuri Slezkine. Chapter 3 starts applying mimetic theory and shows how the theory puts the works of Ferguson and Slezkine in a common perspective. Chapter 4 explores the apocalyptic implications of mimetic theory as exposed in the works of Girard and his scholars and puts them in connection with Massimo Cacciari research around the Apocalypse as anticipated by Saint Paul. Finally, Chapter 5 sketches some lines of further reflection about the meaning of Modernity at large and what it might mean evolving beyond it.

Chapter 1 – The Killer Apps of the West

Niall Ferguson is known for his outspoken views about Western diversity and the primacy of the Western civilization (in particular of its Anglo-Saxon flavor). In his last work "Civilization: West and the Rest" he tries to summarize the key reasons at the heart of this process as well as the lines where the relationship between West and the Rest (with a special attention to China and the Muslim world) might further evolve. Ferguson identifies six core institutions or at least cultural frameworks at the heart of Western primacy and uses each one of them to explain what type of competitive advantage the Anglo-Saxon version of Western civilization gained not only with respect to other civilization but also to other competing variants of the West like for example the French or the Spanish one.

These six "applications" are competition, science, medicine, property rights, consumerism and the ethics of work.

We note incidentally that Ferguson does not mention democracy, freedom, gender equality or any other of the political rights that common rhetoric puts at the center of the founding values of the West. Indeed, if we take the clock back to 1500 none of this was present in European societies while all the other six were to some level starting to appear or in full bloom, so the least we can say is that according to Ferguson liberal democracy is one of the results and not the cause of Western ascent.

In 1500, Europe was a rather depressed area lying at the edge of at least four major Asian empires, that is from West to East the Turkish Ottoman empire, the Persian Safavid dynasty, the Indian Moguls and the Ming of China. All of them outnumbered Europe as a whole both in economic and demographic terms, not to mention each of the single European sovereign entities, that ranged from half-built national states like Spain and France to rich but small regional entities like the Italian Renaissance city states. Europeans had just discovered America, but its exploitation was just at the beginning. Ferguson argues that European fragmentation was exactly the key advantage, because aside from loose cultural obedience to the Pope (that was in any case soon undermined by the Reform) European states and merchants were indeed pushed to fiercely compete between each other while the major concern of all other Asian empires (and especially of China) was rather to dampen internal competition and preserve the status quo. Competition was even fiercer and more ruthless between Europeans themselves, and indeed the history of the Mediterranean conflicts in 1500-1600 shows that the call to European unity against external threats like for example in the battle of Lepanto against the Ottomans was rather the exception in a continuous internal rivalry between the Spaniards and the French or the Genoese and the Venetians to gain the upper hand in the dealings with non-European powers.

This competition led to the continuous development of innovation, both in technology but also in commerce and finance that over the course of time allowed even small European states like Portugal and the Netherlands to be in a position to negotiate with big overseas kingdoms in India and South East Asia. In recalling the Portuguese establishment of their commercial network in South India Ferguson also notes that a crucial role was also played by the willingness of the Europeans to recur to violence on a scale and ruthlessness never seen before. Ferguson uses the China of the Ming dynasty as a contrast because the huge demographic, economic and technology advantage that China had over Europe in 1500 was lost in less than two centuries due to the rigid system setup by the Ming with the good intention to preserve what was by any measure the best and most prosperous empire of the time. But history never stops and 300 years before Hegel explained the role of fight and work in the process of historical transformation the West was embracing competition (sometimes fair but most often deeply unfair) as its development engine.

Yet competition is more of an attitude and has to be sustained at the end also by material means if one has to assert its point of view. And to get to this the second killer app of the West came into play, that is science. In devising the peculiar development that science had in the West, Ferguson compares it to the Muslim world. While from a trade and economic initiative point of view the Muslim powers had nothing to envy to their Western counterparts, acting both as partners and competitors over a millennial trade history, it is on the science side that Islam lost the battle. Again, while other civilizations in 1500 were ahead of the West from a number of scientific and technological standpoints (just think of algebra, entirely imported from Middle East or gunpowder, invented in China), in less than 200 years Western powers and institutions regained all the ground and indeed set the foundations for a primacy that lasts to date.

Unlike in the Muslim world, Western science managed to win its battle for autonomy from religion and set reason free to investigate the causes of a demystified world, or at least a world where Nature was presumed to run on a set of laws accessible to pure human reason. It is well-known that this process was a painful and tortuous one, with ups and downs on both the religious and scientific sides, but to some extent it was also favored by the overall competitive environment so that a scientist having problems in a certain country could always flee to a neighboring state where his activity could find more favor. And while the flourishing of science happened in the modern era, we do not have to forget that key seeds like the institution of universities, that is entities formally independent from both Church and State and devoted to the increase and diffusion of knowledge were indeed laid in the Middle Ages.

With knowledge and science technology quickly followed, and not surprisingly the first applications were in the military. It is around 1500 that a general trend in global trade starts appearing, whereby Western powers import raw materials from outside Europe (e.g. spices and silk from the East, timber and bullion from Americas) and export in exchange manufactured goods, with weapons being the top merchandise. This trend has lasted for more than 500 years and it is being put into question only in these last few decades by the rise of the Asian giants, Japan first and China next.

The third application is medicine and while we can assimilate it to science when it comes to the mental attitude required to research and practice it, actually medicine requires even more determination to challenge myths and any type of religious dogma to make it progress. Ferguson uses medicine also to explain the French variant of Westernization with respect to their approach to colonization. While controlling a colonial empire second only to the British one, the French had, unlike the British, a clear program to assimilate to the ideals of the French Revolution the people they were ruling. While also the British made sure that the ruling local elite would attend higher education in top English schools to establish models, influences and connections, they were never obsessed with the goal of turning each and every member of the Empire in a "citoyen". It does not mean at all that French colonialism was the perfect humanitarian development agency, on the contrary, the generally low if not outright criminal quality of many colonial officers made sure that spoliation and exploitation of colonized people was widespread and continuous. However, documental evidence shows that there was at least a continuous ideal and material effort to bring overseas nations and tribes to the same cultural mindset of the French resident, and the precondition for this was to defend their life and the life of their teachers against the threats of tropical illnesses.

Nowadays this cultural colonization might sound to our politically corrected ears even more suspicious and despicable than the economic one, it is anyway a fact that resources and investment were returned to the colonies to support the basis of their cultural assimilation. In a concession to the dark side of colonization, Ferguson remembers that the Germans used their colonies in Namibia in the early 1900 to test the first concentration camps against the revolted population. He is here maybe taken a bit off track by his Anglo-Saxon pride, as the concentration camps for civilians had been experimented on a large scale by the British troops during the Anglo-Boer war in South Africa a few years earlier, and the British military had in turn applied an invention of the Confederate Army in the American Civil War, whereby tens of thousands of Union prisoners had been gathered in the Andersonville prison camp in Georgia and kept there to starvation. If anything, the Germans copied and gruesomely perfected an Anglo Saxon innovation in warfare.

By comparing the different policies used by European powers in building and managing their colonial empires Niall Ferguson traces to the different legal and economic frameworks for the management of property rights in the Americas the crucial difference between the very different development paths of North and South America. The American colonies gained independence more or less at the same time, between the end of 1700 and the beginning of 1800. All had access to vast spaces and natural resources and all went through their own often bloody internal conflicts, with relatively little levels of interference from their former colonial rulers. And yet, the difference between the US and Canada and, for example, Brazil and Venezuela remains staggering, and cannot be explained alone by the supposedly exploiting policies that the United States increasingly adopted in the course of the 20th century. On the contrary, one can argue with substantial merit that it is exactly this interference that somehow helped narrow the gap, especially after the end of the Cold War.

The ground reason for this according to Ferguson must be traced back to the original setup of property rights established in the colonies. While in Latin America all the land was fundamentally owned by the Spanish and Portuguese Crowns and then farmed out for exploitation (the "encomiendas") to a class of nobles, high officers and court bureaucrats, the English used their North American colonies as a valve to allocate small property lots to scores of immigrants that could not afford a similar fortune in England. Along with this allocation came also the legal system to ensure that property transfers were regulated and enforced, so the market for land property developed. Of course, large landowners soon appeared also in North America (among them, George Washington was known for his vast possession in Virginia) but they were seen as the legitimate result of the dynamics of a market of legally equal and free players and not that of an act of discretion or sheer abuse of a higher authority. Long before the Revolution, the American colonies were made of a large class of property owners that regarded themselves as fully equal in front of the law and were competing with each other under the framework of recognized market rules. The properties of these landowners also included slaves, and one of the reason of the opposition of Confederate states against abrogation was also its clash with one of the founding frameworks of the colonies first and the United States next, that is the intangibility of property rights.

Moving to consumerism, Ferguson defines it as the attitude to let markets decide where to allocate the economic resources, exclusively based on demand and without any additional moral consideration. So if we look at demand, we see that just after or sometimes at the same level of food and shelter the prime demand coming from people is about clothing, with the crucial difference that clothing has much less production and transport constraints than food and shelter and therefore is more open to competition and innovation. Indeed, the growth engine of the Industrial Revolution was the textile industry, whereby British textile manufacturers displaced the competition of the rest of the world in terms of higher quality, dramatically larger volumes and lower unit cost and prices. From this point of view, the main news was rather in the scale than in the industry itself, as textile industry had been the driver of creation and accumulation of European prosperity since the Middle Ages, with Florence and Venice textile manufacturing being

61

progressively displaced by Flanders and later Britain in the world markets. It is also the same trajectory that nowadays is bringing the textile industry and more in general the manufacturing of China to a new level of scale and new productivity gains. And success in core manufacturing also brought along progress and development in machinery, transportation, trade and all its associated services.

In parallel to the development of consumerism there was also the development of an opposite thought calling for the intervention of outside entities (first and foremost the State) into the market to supposedly redress the imbalances that were being produced in terms of resource and income allocations. This trend was eventually epitomized in the half-century long rivalry between the Soviet Union and the United States, and as much as there has never been a perfect Communist regime able to do completely away with private property and markets also the liberal democracies on the opposite side have never given up State intervention to drive their economies in certain ways or others, especially in times of hardship like war or severe economic depression. But if we apply a Hegelian-Marxian criteria to judge history, the least we can say is that the more "consumerism oriented" view of society and economy eventually won on the other one, so, even if far from perfect, it has been able to be more effective in historical terms.

When it comes to work ethics, Ferguson refers openly to Max Weber and his studies on the role of Protestant Reform in the rise and development of modern capitalism. According to Max Weber, one of the key reasons that enabled the rise of Capitalism was the appearance of the protestant ethics of work where the accumulation of capital and business success are actually a moral and religious obligation that the believer has to pursue to make sure he is proceeding on the right track to the salvation of his soul. We have to work for the Other World beyond our death but we know we are on the right track only as much as we are more successful into transforming the earthly World we are living in now according to the generally accepted practice of "business as usual", that is competition and accumulation of capital. Ferguson also complements Weber analysis with the example of modern China and how the diffusion of evangelical Christianity from the early nineteenth century can be directly correlated to economic success, to the extent that today the coastal cities with the highest economic development indexes are often those that show the highest percentage of Christians (it does not matter here if they belong to some kind of State-controlled church or to independent or even prosecuted confessions like the Roman Catholic one).

However, Ferguson also remarks that the influence of Christianity on Chinese society has also been a catastrophic one: it is indeed the first large wave of English missionaries in China in early 1800 that led to the so-called Taiping rebellion whose leaders established an egalitarian theocracy that preaching equality ravaged southern China with bloody revolts between 1850 and 1864, growing the feeling in many Chinese that Christian religion was and is deeply unsuited to Chinese culture (and hence must at least be controlled by the State). In other words, Ferguson highlights but somehow fails to explain the ambiguous effects of Christianity when applied to a traditional culture based on well defined rules to preserve hierarchies and prevent competition from spinning out of control. In a footnote of this chapter, Ferguson also remarks the unusually high success rate of the Jews in embracing the most demanded and typical modern jobs, from industrialist to banker but also opinion leader and scientists of all kinds. It is exactly from this incidental note that Slezkine develops his analysis of the relationship between the Modern Age and the Jewish people.

Chapter 2 – Modernity, or the Jewish Era

Yuri Slezkine is the professor of Soviet history at the University of California, Berkeley and has become known beyond academia with his 2003 book "The Jewish Century" where he gives a new interpretation of the role of the Jews in Russian history and more in general in the Modern era. Slezkine structures his analysis in four parts: in the first part, he defines the Jews as one example of a broader anthropological category that he calls the "Mercurial minorities". In the second part, he describes more in detail the interaction between the Jews and the processes that created the modern era, enriching the perspective of Niall Ferguson. In the third and fourth part, Slezkine finally studies in detail the contribution of the Jews to the Russian Revolution and the different attitudes they took in the 20th century in response to the developments of Capitalism, Nationalism and Soviet Communism.

Before proceeding, let's recall the general caveat that his research must definitely not be applied to the individual Jew and not even to the majority of Jews but is rather referring to historical trends, ways of thinking and roles that appeared in Jewish people with far more statistical frequency than in others. Back to the first part, Slezkine starts by noting that it is a common pattern of all civilizations to have ethnic minorities dedicated to manage certain particular sectors of economy like trade, finance, craftsmanship but also higher liberal professions like medicine and law so that from this point of view the Jews are no exception but have to be rather classified together with similar minorities like the Mon of Thailand, the Parsi and the Jain of India, the Armenians of the Ottoman Empire, the Gypsies in Central Europe, the Inandan of Sahara, the Chinese of South East Asia, the Lebanese and Levant minorities of Latin America and West Africa or the Russian Germans in Czarist Russia.

Slezkine therefore defines a broader classifications of people between "Mercurians" and "Apollineans", after the two Greek gods Apollo and Mercury. Apollineans are tied to a very specific geographic place and have a very strong sense of their homeland and their kinship, Mercurians see themselves as not linked to a particular country and mobile by definition, ready to change place if the opportunity or the need arises. Apollineans tend to privilege farming, primary production and all occupations linked to statehood, first and foremost warfare, and measure their success and status in a broad sense on "quantity" (of land, authority, reputation, etc.) to establish hierarchies. Mercurians, on the other hand, have to rely on Apollineans for primary production in exchange for services and secondary manufacturing and crafts. They have to rely on their intelligence and have to appeal to relations and quality to assert their point of view. If Apollineans cultivate fields, Mercurians grow human relations, where Apollineans have duties and obligations that tie them to a specific group Mercurians deliberately set themselves out of the main tribes to be in a position to negotiate between different ones. As Mercurians live in the middle of much bigger and powerful majorities, they have to protect their existence mainly by erecting cultural barriers,that basically means enforcing sexual segregation, adopt rigorous dietary and behavioral codes of conduct and have one or more internal languages to shield their culture from external contamination. The multiple language capability and the consequent higher literacy rate further increase the gap of Mercurians in mediation and interpretation skills with respect to Apollineans. And while Apollineans understand fellow Apollineans, each Mercurial kin is alone on its own, all the rest of the world being simply "goy" (for the Jews) or "gadjo" (for the Gypsies).

This radical diversity has always been remarked by the two groups and over the centuries Apollineans and Mercurians have never liked each other on the very accurate ground that they perceive their radical difference, and Mercurians have always known they would be those with far more to lose in a clash, tolerated by Apollineans only as long as their services would be useful and necessary. The fact that the unlucky ones have been the Mercurians is so obvious that in many of the myths about their origins there is some misdeed that condemned them to their Diaspora lives (e.g. the Gypsies believe they were condemned by God to perpetual exile for making the nails used to crucify Jesus).

In some respect, Slezkine definition recalls the one of Carl Schmitt between the "peoples of the Land" and the "peoples of the Sea", but while the latter was defining this concept with the perspective of the clash between Germany and England, Slezkine is trying to extend the difference beyond politics and into anthropology. After this general introduction, Slezkine moves to the specific case of the Jews, who have been for many centuries, more or less happily, nothing more than the Mercurians of Christianity, so familiar to the extent of sharing most of the Scriptures and a good chunk of the transcendental beliefs of their host populations and yet absolutely focused on preserving their diversity. Things start to change exactly with the arrival of modernity, or, to use the chronology of Ferguson, when the West starts developing its killer applications.

In the perspective of Slezkine, the birth of modernity is the beginning of a process where the Apollinean nations of Europe have become increasingly mobile, involved in trade, fascinated by the intellectual challenges of science, in short they have started to morph into Mercurians, and more particularly into Jews. In agreement with Ferguson (and scores of other historians) Slezkine identifies Christian Reform and the birth of the sovereign national State as a key step in this direction, but while Ferguson remains in an economic and legal perspective Slezkine adds a cultural and anthropological point of view. Reform put believers in a situation where their salvation was depending more and more on the study and interpretation of the Holy Scripture and compliance to strict codes of conduct rather than joining the "happily sinful" Catholic community where priests and maybe the occasional miracle would guarantee salvation for all.

As Slezkine colorfully puts it, Puritans were turning into something similar to Jews with the pig and conversely Jews could be seen as Puritans without the pig. But while Jews could rely heavily on strong family and tribal ties to help them along their spiritual and social Diasporas, in what type of tribe could the new, independent modern European man find the support he needed when the wars of religion started to tear apart the Middle Age Christianity? The answer came with the development of the sovereign national State, that among many other things set the scene for universal Mercurialism because it transformed on a national scale Apollinean peasants into Mercurial traders. Just like any Mercurial tribe, every new nation would have its own language able to address both the sacred and secular aspects of life, a reference narrative describing its genesis and a destiny to pursue among all other "strangers" that would irremediably remain an overwhelming majority with which the new universal Mercurial nations would have to deal with the classic Apollinean ways of warfare and domination if possible but most often with the typical Mercurial techniques of mediation and negotiation.

This transformation needed three ingredients: a foundation epic or poem written in the national language (that would gain literary dignity through this very same work), a prophet or a Bard that would make the Nation aware of its fate (almost always the author of the previous narrative) and a new State (quite often pre-existent and eager to gain additional legitimacy) that would preserve and promote this new secular religion in a potentially hostile environment.

Even from this very different framework, Slezkine shares the conclusions of Ferguson that Reform Anglo-Saxon countries (that is, England) have been more effective in implementing the model than continental ones, especially France, where an honest worshipping of the "nation as is" was deemed not enough and reinforced with the supplemental invention of the Universal Reason, so that the French had to learn to be also universal citizens, or in other words better universal Mercurians. This new inventions of modernity initially benefited the Jews, that prospered in a world where their millennia-old Mercurial skills where in increasing demand and they were soon trying to join the new national churches, that seemed at least less demanding in their admission requirements, as the new State did not ask for a full apostasy from their religion like ancient Christianity did. As a consequence, many Jews embarked on the assimilation journey with a fervor in the new liberal-national world that was unmatched by their fellow Apollinean peasants, and they became at once the symbol of the new era and of the difficulties to adapt to it, because unlike the less skilled Apollineans they did not physically belong to the new religion even if no one could interpret its spirit better than they did.

Jews were many of the biggest bankers, lawyers and scientists, as a similar set of statistics reported by Slezkine complements the one presented by Ferguson, and Jews were also some of the greatest poets of the modern "malaise", among those we recall just Kafka, Proust (the christened son of a liberal, assimilated Jewish mother) and the Leopold Bloom portrayed by Joyce in the "Ulysses". In parallel to Nationalism, that was trying to persuade peasants that the city ruled by state laws and thriving on a free market economy was just a bigger and better version of their old village, two other religions eventually appeared with the clear intention to address the loneliness and displacement of modern mankind.

These were Marxism and Freudism, and to both of them Jewish intellectual gave major contributions. Marxism placed the original sin of modernity in the division of work that could be redeemed only by a collective salvation at the end of history, where capitalism would eventually be toppled in an apocalyptic catharsis carried out by the poor masses of proletarians. Freudism placed instead the origin of evil in a duality within the individual itself between the rational ego and the unconscious that cannot be resolved but rather come to terms with, exclusively with the help of qualified professionals engaged in a service relationship. Freudism does not guarantee salvation of souls but can help in reaching peace of mind in living in a complex society. Both religions also made extensive usage of the latest scientific findings in economics and medicine and both shared a "bootstrap" origin: as much as Marx had been able to self-transcend himself above the flow of history and describe its evolution laws and eventual outcome, so Freud had been able to self-analyze his psyche without any external aid. The new beliefs also rejected Nationalism as a way to address the unhappiness of modern Apollineans and their claim to have a better solution to the problem of modernity able to resolve at once individual and collective conflicts was strong enough to legitimize the birth of new States (first and foremost the Soviet Union) or the expansion of the liberal state into the sphere of the psychological well-being of its citizens like in the United States.

Interestingly enough, both Freudism and Marxism saw the deep connection between modernity and the Jews: if Freud considered psychoanalysis as "mostly a Jewish issue", Marx predicted that the Jewish spirit would eventually disappear with Capitalism, as the essence of the Jewish people was nothing more than embodying the mercantile spirit.

The rejection of nationalism in the name of a higher common instance attracted lots of lonely, displaced tribal Mercurians to the two new modern religions, and Slezkine documents with impressive data the large contribution given by young Jews to the birth, growth and eventual success of the Soviet Revolution. It was a generation that rejected the tradition of their fathers because they were guilty of embodying the cold spirit of modernity. But the goal of their fathers had been nothing more than to prepare them to join one of the national tribes that were being formed and become Apollineans like the others.

Isaac Babel', who described his participation to the Russian-Polish war as active Red Army member in the "Red

Cavalry" novel, is a good example of this trajectory. He was born in 1894 in Odessa, the son of a relatively successful grain trader that, in the very same words of his sister, was wishing for his offspring a future of success and study. Actually, here the Jews were setting themselves apart from last minute universal Mercurians, as for them success was a precondition to reach true knowledge and not the other way round like for transformed Apollineans. Statistics show that the sons of successful Jewish bankers and businessmen increasingly enrolled in liberal arts and pure science faculties. And in these positions they often became political radicals or critics of the establishment, committing themselves to the most powerful reactions to Modernity with the help of all the modern tools developed in thousands of years of Mercurial life.

Isaac Babel' became first a perfect Russian, assimilating Pushkin with far more enthusiasm than the Torah and eventually joined the Communist Party. In a prophetic conversation that Babel' has with a Ukrainian landlord about the Jews, he is asked how many Jews live in Eastern Europe. "Around ten million" answers Babel'. "At the end of these wars, no more than two hundred thousand will survive. You know why? They are hated by both of us". The Jews were hated by the anti-Communist landlords and peasants for they represented Mercurial modernity and at the same time they would be hated by the new Communist regime as soon as it would realize they represented at once yet another foreign power, Israel and the intellectual and business backbone of America, its most formidable rival. Babel' did not live enough to witness this twist of history as he was executed in the purges of 1939. Jews also elaborated their own kind of nationalism, in the Yiddish and Hebrew variant that later led to Zionism. It was a very particular nationalism, as it had to transform a people of millennial Mercurians into a small nation of Apollinean peasants, considering in the process as invaders the resident Apollinean peasants of Palestine.

But as the Jews were practicing one of the most eccentric nationalisms ever developed, another one had appeared that identified all the problems of modernity simply and brutally with the existence of the Jews. Quoting Slezkine "in Germany, the tax collector, the league student, the meaningless bureaucrat, the nitpicking teacher and the dumb peasant were able to rebel against the unbearable requirements of modernity by identifying them with the Jews and setting up the biggest, best organized and brutal pogrom of history. In Russia, the sons of the intelligentsia (many of whom Jews) took power and tried to implement the most perfect Universal Citizen ever dreamed since the French Revolution by setting up the most violent and brutal attack against the tax collector, the league student, the meaningless bureaucrat, the nitpicking teacher and the dumb peasant. Specially the dumb peasant."

So in the 20th century the history of the Jews (and of the Modern world) has become the history of one Hell and the pilgrimage to three promised lands, namely Soviet Union, the United States and Israel. Slezkine dedicates the third and fourth part of his book to explain in detail the role of the Jews in the Russian Revolution and how they instead fared to the other two promised lands that opened to them early in the 20th century. One great credit that Slezkine has is undoubtedly to bring to the general attention the fact that for the whole first half of the 1900 the best perspectives for the Jews were presented not by the United States but rather by the cosmopolitan and egalitarian society of the Soviet Union. It is well-known the success the Jews immigrants and their descendants have had in America and the role they played in building the Pantheon of the American imagination: Superman, Spider Man, Capitan America belong all to the genius of Jewish immigrants, mostly from Eastern Europe, that in perfect Mercurial style first changed and localized their names before interpreting their new homeland in the Thirties and Forties of the last century, not to mention the global expression of "dark side" that is the literal translation of the "sitra achra" or other side concept of the Kabbalah.

A little less known is that Jewish intellectuals, engineers and managers also provided a large fraction of the education, production and administrative machine of the Soviet Union, always in much higher proportion compared to the rest of the population. One can agree or not with the historical fresco of Slezkine and his line of interpretation, yet with respect to Ferguson he brings the analysis one step further as he identifies Western modernity as a single process (the embracing of

Mercurial habits on a global scale) that besides an amazing success at increasing overall prosperity and well being (the aspects upon which Niall Ferguson insists) it also created a huge reaction and is still perceived as "unfair" and "unnatural" or outright "evil", both outside and inside Western civilization. For the reasons we have explained, Jews did not actually invented it but where somehow always involved in all the key crossroads of its creation and even more in all the attempts to overcome it. But why exactly have Europeans started the process to become universal Mercurians and developed the national State and the free market as by products? And what is exactly behind Mercurialism, beyond the vivid and insightful analogies provided by Slezkine? It is now time to introduce mimetic theory to shed new light over that two centuries between Renaissance and Reform.

Chapter 3 – Markets, State and the Containment of Desire

Before connecting the first set of dots between the works of Slezkine and Ferguson, I recall quickly the core principles of mimetic theory as perfected by René Girard and his school since the early 1960. For a systematic description I refer the interested reader to the first chapters of "Things hidden from the foundation of the world". In line with a philosophical tradition that starts from Hegel and continues to modern existentialism and psychoanalysis, Girard recognizes desire as one of the key differentiator (if not the only one) between mankind and animals. We do not delve here on the precise definition of desire, suffice it to say that desire has not to be mistaken with need (like the need for food and shelter common to every living being) nor with instinct (which, taking for example the most famous one, the sexual instinct, is an internal drive of the behavior of living beings with a clear and defined object that can satisfy it).

Both needs and instincts have well defined objects that can quell their push, and we note incidentally that while people cannot last much time without fulfilling needs, the same does not apply to instincts whose satisfaction can be postponed almost indefinitely without jeopardizing the basic living functions. Desire, notes Girard in the wake of Hegel and his followers (most notably, we refer to the interpretation of Alexandre Kojeve) does not have a specific object, in the sense that it can take any object as its content (a woman, a flag, a social position). In addition to that, Girard remarks also the mimetic nature of desire, that is the trend of people to imitate each other's desires or in other words we desire the most disparate things just because other people do it, regardless of their objective utility. So what? After all, this is exactly what every kindergarten teacher or parents with small children know very well, without going to philosophy classes.

The value of mimetic theory is to be very consequent with the implications of this basic finding that is in other words the triangular nature of desire. According to mimetic theory, there is no such thing as a direct link between the desired object and the one who desires, but there is always a third person, the mediator, to whom people look to know what to desire. Mediation of desire can in turn be classified in two categories, external and internal mediation. External mediation is when for whatever reason the mediator is perceived as belonging to a complete different class by the one who desires and is therefore not perceived as a rival and this typically leads to positive emulation. This is what happens for example between an extraordinarily gifted teacher and his pupils, or between a saint and his followers. Internal mediation instead arises when the one who desires sees her mediator on the same level as hers, with no special rights on the common desired object. But if we are bound to crave the same objects and we see ourselves as equals, rivalry and conflict are inherent dynamics of human interaction and if we project that back in stone age (assuming this dynamic of desire is already in place) we need to figure out a mechanism to control rivalry if we do not want to run the risk of violent escalations that could lead to the self-destruction of human communities.

Mimetic theory identifies that in the scapegoat mechanism, whereby all the tensions are transferred to one of the member of the community and discharged via its elimination, with the perfect good faith of all the remaining members that the victim is really guilty of all the evil that is ravaging the group. The member of the community can be human or animal and its elimination physical or symbolic, in general over the evolution of mankind we move from the physical elimination of people to the symbolic expulsion of animals or things, albeit with frequent setbacks from the most evolved versions to their gruesome ancestors. Mimetic theory eventually provides a scientific explanation for the origin of religion and a number of phenomena linked to it (from the centrality of sacrifice in every religion to the common structure of mythical narrative that can be traced in cultures as far away as Ancient Greeks and Native Polynesians).

In the most recent development, Girard and his scholars have started to apply mimetic theory also to the explanation of historical and economic processes. However, far from trying to become a "theory of everything human" (that have a regrettable tendency to develop into totalitarian ideologies), mimetic theory openly declares its limits and domain of applicability. While dealing with inter-individual relationship, ("interdividual" in the theory jargon), mimetic theory clearly says it does not provide an explanation nor a model for fundamental modes of interaction of people like love and parent-child relationship, unless for some well defined pathological forms like jealousy and the "double bind" phenomena observed in the development of schizophrenia.

Let's now move back to interpreting Slezkine and Ferguson in "mimetic light". The observations of Slezkine around Mercurians and Apollineans have a straightforward mimetic interpretation. If we consider more in detail the typical activities of the Mercurians, they all have to do with tasks that, while essential to the broader community, involve a greater risk of igniting rivalry and conflict because they are all about mediation that can spark both positive and negative imitation. Trade is by definition based on comparisons and competition. Lawyers thrive in the resolution of conflicts. Doctors often deal with extreme pain and grief situations, that especially in ancient societies tend to border with sorcery and jinx. Also certain kinds of craftsmanship like blacksmiths potently recall contagious violence with their tools and artifacts. And finally, nothing like money can spark envy and resentment and has therefore to be managed particularly carefully and, so to say, professionally.

Apollineans instead work within well defined boundaries, shielded by the effects of other people's envy by their established rights over land and property that are in turn guaranteed by the State, or, in ancient society, by the belonging to a group or tribe that provides a set of guarantees and obligations to its members. Enjoying the protection of a tribe means also being ready to join in retaliation if some of the members has suffered any harm. The different symbiotic societies that Slezkine describes (the Parsi of India, the Mon of Thailand, and of course the Jews of the West), separated from a geographic, temporal and cultural point of view, can be traced back by mimetic theory to the same model where a broader, stronger community farms out mimetically dangerous jobs to a minority that is tolerated in good times and can be used as scapegoat during bad ones.

A chilling precursor of this habit has been observed in some Amazonian tribes, where few prisoners of war are selected to live within a community only to be sacrificed if the need arises (e.g. to quell conflicts internal to the tribe or as preparation of a new war). Mimetic theory also provides at least the beginning of a scientific answer to the question that haunted religion scholars over the past 200 years, that is if and what there is a radical difference between the Judeo-Christian tradition and all other religions. Mimetic theory asserts that the difference exists, and it lies in the full revelation of the scapegoat mechanism that other religions tend to conceal. Unlike all other myths, the Bible and the Gospel systematically side with the victims and this revelation peaks with the accounting of the Passion of Jesus. Whether you believe or not in Resurrection, by reading the accounts of the Passion no one can have the least doubt of who the bad guys are, or actually that everybody is a bad guy except the one that is condemned to death so that "all the rest can survive".

Read instead the Oedipus, and it is apparent that all the evils that plague the city of Thebes are the effect of the impious Oedipus, who killed the father and married his mother, and of no one else. But by revealing the mechanism that has kept ancient communities together, Judeo-Christian tradition also opens the door to unlimited competition, escalation, and ultimately violence because scapegoating requires that people that benefit from it are fully unaware of its dynamics. The very same fact that we call somebody or something a scapegoat means that we do not really believe in it and therefore its effects in terms of containment of rivalry and conflict will be ultimately limited. In other words, if we want to fully unleash competition, the first thing we have to do is to remove the religious and mythical barriers to it, and this is exactly what the Bible and the Gospels do. We do not mean at all that the Judeo-Christian scripture is an hymn to capitalism and free market, as it is full of warnings against the pitfalls of mimetic desire.

What mimetic theory asserts is that the Western Holy Scripture is grounded in an anthropology framework that does not hide the very human causes of violence, rivalry and conflict and progressively erodes the effectiveness of the system of the "sacred" that was used by mankind as a way to externalize violence. Between Renaissance and Reform, it was apparent that while the old gods had lost their authority after 1000 years of Christianity, this very same Christianity, torn apart in the bloodshed of the wars of religion and the rush to conquer new spaces was also far away from being the Kingdom of God.

What emerged, from a mimetic point of view, was a new model where scarcity replaced the sacred. And as much as the sacred is not an institution but rather the mould of ancient institutions, so scarcity turned out to be the mould of modern institutions. If scapegoating does no longer work, and the sacred is progressively voided of its force, individuals progressively lose the obligations that tie them to their tribe, restricting them to close relatives. Where there used to be the risk of large public rivalries and conflicts that could extend to the whole community, there is now a multitude of private mimetic conflicts that do not spread thanks to the loosened tribal ties but these background conflicts give the evidence that it is very difficult, actually impossible to satisfy the desires and maybe even the needs of everyone.

So, not recognizing the mimetic origin of desire, modernity found universal scarcity as the sole possible explanation. We all crave for someone else's things, and we observe that in the long run (and even with increased income) the situation does not change. If we still do not recognize the mechanism of desire, the obvious conclusion is that there are not enough resources to make us all happy. The most efficient management of scarcity, as economic theory and the history of the West show, requires the setup of a market regulated by prices for resources to be optimally allocated, a legal system to transfer property rights of goods and a State empowered to enforce all this on a reasonably large area.

The "invention" or "discovery" of sacred and scarcity are just two different and mutually exclusive mimetic modes that people have found to deal with the unpleasant effects of mimetic desire. The sacred applies to traditional societies where violence is contained (in the sense of limited) in terms of prohibitions and rituals and it contains (in the sense of using) violence in the sacrifice of the scapegoat. Scarcity appears in societies that reject sacrifice as mechanism of regulation and limit violence by privatizing conflicts and removing sacred ties between the vast majority of their members. However, scarcity-based societies see the appearance of replacement victims in the masses of those who lose their private battles and are progressively excluded from social and economic life by the indifference of the other players.

We do not mean at all that scarcity is purely a cultural invention, as there are scores of situations where real scarcity of primary goods arises. It is interesting to compare how traditional and modern societies react to the most typical case of scarcity, that is famine. Ritual and tribal obligations of traditional societies would mandate the better off to start sharing their reserve of food with the less fortunate, that in turn would be regulated by the very same system to kind of moderate their requests. Failure to comply with the rules would entail the risk of triggering a mimetic crisis to which the only answer of the community would be the sacrifice. As the famine worsens, mimetic crises progressively select new victims freeing up more resources for those left until the famine is over. The victim selection process might be coded in some ritual or happen on a random basis (most likely, it would start in a somehow orderly form and become increasingly random with the progressive collapse of the social order), eventually the survivors would be a set made mostly of members of the ruling class and a variety of clever, ruthless and outright lucky members of other classes. For the survivors, the victim would have been the price to pay to satisfy the wrath of the gods.

In modern society, the onset of famine sends the price of food skyrocketing, with the poor being progressively left to starvation and also some of the rich if famine continues to stress the social structure beyond the point where enforcement of mutual indifference by law can no longer be guaranteed. The final outcome of severe famine does not differ much from that of traditional societies that is survivors would most likely be members of the ruling class plus the fittest of the lower classes. Survivors again would look back and wonder whether all had been done to minimize the number of victims. After all, two thousand years of Christianity did not pass in vain and at least the scandal for unjustified sacrifice and a compassion for the explicit victim have somehow engrained in the Western attitude. In both cases, the survivors would be fully justified or at least relieved of their sense of guilt as the victims "deserved" to be sacrificed in traditional society or there "was nothing more we could do" for them in modern society.

In real life crises, what tends to happen is a mix of the two, with the State acting as a surrogate of the tribal system as correctly pointed out by Slezkine. As we have the co-existence of two modes of social mimesis that are mutually exclusive in organizing society in normal times, it is clear that the debate that always ensues of whether the famine was exacerbated by the avidity of grain merchants or by the incompetence of the public authority that meddled with market laws and prevented optimal resource allocation is somehow meaningless.

We can now read all the killer apps enumerated by Niall Ferguson as consequences of the shift of Western societies from "sacred mode" to "scarcity mode", or, to put it in Slezkine terminology, from "Apollinean" mode to "Mercurial" mode. Finally, moving from traditional to modern society also changed the meaning of solidarity. Far from being an uncontrolled outbreak of social Darwinism, liberalism started with a deep interest for interaction between individuals, to the extent that Adam Smith considered far more important his "Theory of moral sentiments" with respect to the much more famous "Wealth of Nations". Indeed, for Adam Smith individuals have a natural tendency to empathy and look for other people empathy and approval when it comes to moral evaluation of actions. And while solidarity in traditional societies is more of a social obligation enforced by the system of rituals and prohibitions, in modern society it is a prize that must be gained every day by means of an honorable and gentle interaction with other people, and this conduct, as Benjamin Franklin noted, is also the one that makes us look reliable from a business perspective.

Regardless of the fact that we might be driven by the private vices of Mandeville, when it comes to action we always consider the judgment of the "man without" of Adam Smith and this shapes us in a form that helps build public virtues and increase the overall wealth of the nation. The irony in this process is that the mimetic nature of desire remained largely misunderstood, at least to the large majority of people and this happened despite the fact that many of the Bards of the modern nations, from Dante to Shakespeare and Cervantes have instead developed a very precise and accurate theory of mimetic desire in their masterpieces. René Girard himself first discovered and explained mimetic desire in literature in his seminal work "Desire, Deceit and the novel", and later extended its research to the Sacred and primitive society.

The establishment of modernity on a base that still left hidden or misunderstood the true nature of human desire also had detrimental effects on all the doctrines that tried to diagnose and overcome its illnesses. From a mimetic perspective, Marxism simply chose to take the world back in the era of the sacred solidarity, failing to understand that this was not primarily a problem of wrong allocation of the means of production or excessive amount of religious opium in the air, but that simply after 2000 years of Christianity it was impossible to really believe in the value of sacrifice, even if they were carried out on a collective scale exterminating peasants or by making sure that in purge trials the prosecuted himself would admit his guilt. In other words, Marxism did not realize that not all religions were opium, and rather there was one tradition that albeit with varying degrees of success was curing people from the sacrificial hangover. "Property is sacred" has been the foundation of the modern world, and Marx thought that the sacred was a relic on the way of a quick dismissal and focused his attention on the fight to overcome property. He should have done the opposite.

On the other hand, Freudism started from the intuition that it was more of an inner problem of man rather than social organization. The core finding of Freudism, the Oedipus complex, correctly identified that there were three elements in the human problem but somehow it restricted the area to sexuality and parental relations. In "Violence and the Sacred" Girard shows how Freud when so close to capturing the real nature of desire with the Oedipus and the origin of myths and rituals in "Totem and Taboos" but somehow fell prey to the Romantic belief that there is nothing between myself and my desired object.

According to Freud, the child really desires his mother (albeit with his unconscious part), while for Girard rivalry with the father could be sparked by any object, provided that there are the conditions for internal mediation. Ironically, as Slezkine remarks, both Marxism and Freudism can be explained in term of the other doctrine: in Freudian terms, Marxism is the result of the rejection of the spiritual father and in Marxist terms, Freudism is the perfect bourgeois ideological superstructure that overlooks the underlying structures. In his last book "Battling to the end" Girard tries to apply his theory to history, putting it on a par with all the other visions of history that have so far tried to capture the trends of human evolution in general and of modernity and post-modernity in particular. Girard starts his analysis from "On war", the treaty of Carl von Clausewitz that appeared shortly after the end of the Napoleon wars in 1830, just about in the same place and time where Hegel was finalizing his grand vision of history as the process bound to find a happy end through continuous strife and violence that would also greatly influence Marx.

As J.P. Dupuy shows in his essays about liberalism, a similar optimism is also shared by the liberal thought, like for example Von Hayek, although obviously the happy end at the end of history will be reached with entirely different means and policies than those predicated by Socialism. Girard on the contrary endorses the mimetic intuitions of Clausewitz and his pessimistic vision that politics and war are ultimately regulated by mimetic rivalry and nothing prevents this rivalry from escalating without limits. Market and State contained Armageddon or the dynamic of uncontained escalation, all across the course of modernity. State has become more totalitarian in the sense that it extended well beyond the initial scope of the "night watch state" to the oversized dimension of the welfare state-society. Markets have become increasingly efficient and global, with the biggest companies able to rival with States in terms of power and influence. Both have initiated a rush to increase indefinitely their size, power, reach and relevance in individual lives and claim to represent the ultimate achievement of history. As Carl Schmitt pointed out, this giant escalation led ultimately to the World Wars of last century and recurring economic shocks of ever greater magnitude that four centuries after the European wars of religion left the founding structures of modernity alive but delegitimized. Carl Schmitt himself was speaking with direct knowledge of the matter as he had a role in justifying this rush by providing the philosophical and legal framework to the ascent to power of Hitler.

According to Girard we are therefore living in an ambiguous world that, while undoubtedly growing more aware and better at saving victims in increasing numbers, it counterbalances this trend with the relentless destruction of the traditional brakes to the escalation of violence and the increased power and availability of the means of destruction. It is not by chance that René Girard puts at the beginning of his last work a quote from the "Lettres provinciales" of Blaise Pascal: "All the efforts of violence cannot weaken truth, and they only make it more apparent. At the same time, all the light of truth cannot stop violence and it only irritates and exacerbates it more". So for Girard it is very likely that at the end of history mankind will be trapped in an Apocalypse that will be entirely of its own making. It is now time to have a closer look at Armageddon and we start by reporting on the work of Massimo Cacciari about the first reference to the end of times made by Saint Paul in his epistles.

Chapter 4 – The Network of the Antichrist

In the second letter to the Thessalonians, one of the first Christian communities that he founded, Saint Paul makes a statement about the end of time and history that has challenged and baffled interpreters for two thousand years.

Saint Paul writes to his disciples that are divided over whether the second coming of Jesus is imminent, and with it the end of this world. It is a quite widespread belief in early Christianity and it is incidentally also one of the reasons that have pushed Saint Peter to leave Jerusalem and eventually move to Rome, as Jesus was expected by some prophecies to appear there. In his epistle, Saint Paul clearly states that the end of times is not yet close, as the end of time will be the age of the Antichrist but before the Antichrist comes, the "power that restraints it" must be removed. Literally, "for the mystery of Lawlessness is already at work, but only until the one who now restraints it is removed". What is this restraining power, the "katechon" in the Greek version of the text?

For early Christian interpreters, among which Saint Augustine, the katechon is an implicit reference to the Roman Empire. Disorder cannot conquer the Ancient World until the Roman Empire oversees its functioning, and Saint Paul, according to this interpretation, simply does not want to explicitly predict the end of the Roman Empire as this risks bringing the early Christian community to the attention or worse the hostility of public authorities. After the fall of the Roman Empire, and the enduring absence of the Antichrist, the katechon has been re-interpreted by various commentators to the closest entity that was in some ways ensuring law and order in the secular world.

In a brilliant paper, Wolfgang Palaver, one of the most respected Girardian scholars, shows that also the Leviathan of Thomas Hobbes can be interpreted as a secular "katechon". In 1600, in a Europe devastated by religious conflicts between Catholics, Protestants and various denominations of Reformed churches, the work of jurists like Grotius and De Victoria and philosophers like Hobbes lies the foundation for the birth of the absolute sovereign State, the last entity that ensures that the world does not fall into an uncontrolled and unrestrained apocalyptic war. The breeding of the absolute sovereign State with the concept of nation soon leads to the modern variation of tribalism highlighted by Slezkine, or the nation State, that, in turn, has taken us very close to Armageddon in the last world wars of the last century.

As Carl Schmitt points out in his masterpiece "The nomos of the Earth", after 1945 we continue to use the political concepts put together in 1600 but somehow this framework is now void of meaning and creaks continue to appear and undermine it. We quote as example the asymmetric wars waged by terror groups on traditional States, the unconventional answers put in place by the latter to respond to the threat (e.g. the doctrine of the United States to strike their presumed enemies irrespective of the borders that might shield them) but also the growing level of interaction and conflicts between sovereign entities and financial institutions that have grown up to sovereign entities in their own right, like for example the European Central Bank or the International Monetary Fund.

It is in this line of reflection that Massimo Cacciari casts his considerations on the katechon. After recalling the history of the interpretations of the katechon, Cacciari remarks that the "lawlessness" ("anomos" in ancient Greek) that characterizes the Antichristian time is not necessarily a synonym of "chaos", "anarchy", destruction and all the images we usually associate with the end of times. On the contrary, the time of the Antichrist is a time where a new order must be established, an order that finally rejects "forever" the message of Christianity. As such, it is a time that must by definition aspire to be eternal and therefore cannot be grounded on complete war and destruction. It is the time where every transcendence is denied and, as Hegel first and Nietzsche next prophesized, the last man eventually finds in himself and for himself all the reasons for its satisfaction. It is the time where all authorities are rejected, including the authority of the homogenous universal State imagined by Hegel, as the only political reality recognized by the last man is his unlimited will to satisfy his desires just because he can do it.

Law and State become mere ways to discipline everyone's exercise of absolute authority to maximize satisfaction, kind of traffic lights needed to manage the crowds that want to flock to the occasional beach, funfair or rave party. It is not a lone man the one that occupies this place of history, on the contrary, if one object symbolizes his condition it is the one of the network, where each node points to another one without any possibility of transcendence, and even more important, no need for it as the network can expand indefinitely and self-create and satisfy all its needs. Cacciari recalls here the reflections of Solov'ev and other Russian philosophers of the early 1900 that imagined the time of Armageddon not necessarily as an era of continuous destruction but rather one of quiet satisfaction, and "Placidus" is the name that identifies the spirit of the Antichrist. In post-modernity, well being and freedom become the ultimate goal of individuals and consequently economic and political structures are increasingly judged by the ability to serve this purpose.

Far from having only a material definition (like for example access to natural resources or lack of political oppression), well-being and freedom also point to a spiritual dimension where they mean the possibility of ever increasing satisfaction of ever increasing desires of all kinds, not least the desire of recognition. If Andy Warhol was envisaging in the 1960s an era where each one could aspire to fifteen minutes of celebrity, today social media prosper on the promise that everyone has a chance of being liked by the rest of mankind.

It is interesting to note that mimetic theory lends itself to a double interpretation, depending if we want to endorse the immanent or transcendentalist approach to the "katechon" and the end of time. René Girard opted for the transcendentalist approach, and converted to Christianity while studying mimetic desire. Girard openly declared throughout his career that, while using a rigorously scientific method, one could see mimetic theory as an "anthropological apology" of Christianity in general and Roman Catholicism in particular. This has drawn to him at once the hostility of non-religious scholars that considered him a theologian in disguise and also of full-service theologians that considered his theory as an attempt to rationalize and scientifically explain faith and religion. As Girard points out, given the self-referential and hidden nature of the scapegoat mechanism, only a Revelation from God can set man free from its trap.

But mankind has repeatedly rejected to fully embrace Christianity, in all its ancient, Middle Age and modern varieties, so the result is that we are at the mercy of unleashed mimetic rivalry that will ultimately wipe away all the structures elaborated over time to restrain it. We see that State and Market, the two structures emerged in modernity to replace mythological structures eroded by Christianity are increasingly losing legitimacy and hence restraining power. We do not know if a new restraining structure will emerge, if not the time of Lawlessness is close to arrive.

This might not be such a bad thing, according to a non-religious or outright atheist interpretation of mimetic theory. If we assume that mankind is based on mimetic desire and we are alone on this rock in the middle of the universe, it was only a question of time and statistical probability for one of the tribes that appeared over the planet to start getting the right reading of the scapegoat mechanism. First, the scapegoat mechanism would defend early human communities against self-destruction. Then, over time and with a bit of luck, one of these communities would eventually get the right interpretation and take humanity to the next step. By pure chance, this tribe happened to be the Jews, and the Jew that came out with the perfect interpretation was so successful to be rejected by his own people, proof that indeed a step change in understanding had taken place. From this point of view, the trajectory is set and "Lawlessness" is indeed the final paradise.

Like in the Hegelian perspective, we know what man will look like in the end of time, and we know that the process is painful. Unlike in Marx and Hegel, we have objectively less reasons to be optimistic that mankind will eventually get to that point or rather get the situation irremediably out of control in the middle journey for having removed the brakes too early or too abruptly. There is no scientific or rational way to judge which one of the two interpretations is true, as choosing between the two is indeed a decision grounded in freedom, just like choosing to adhere to a faith or not. Nonetheless, moving the timeline back to present day from the end of time, both visions lead to interesting and novel interpretations on how and where modernity might evolve. We will highlight some points of further reflection in the next chapter, focusing on the nature of contemporary conflicts, the new concepts that have to become common sense in the public debate to tackle the new challenges and possibly the new potential "katechons" that might frame a new era after Modernity.

Chapter 5 – Containing Armageddon 2.0

The Armageddon is the time where irresolvable conflicts appear, and they are irresolvable because they belong to essentially different types. There are "sacrificial" conflicts, typical of the pre-modern era, that are ultimately governed and contained by the laws of sacrifice. Modernity invented the "scarcity" conflict, and created the framework to contain it with the property and sovereignty concepts. As Carl Schmitt pointed out, the difference was so radical that the Europeans, while considering all other European states as peers, they would consider the rest of the world (with the exception of the Turkish empire) as open land for conquest until in the post-colonial era the sovereign state concept has been universally adopted. Then, starting from the second half of last century, a new type of conflict has appeared, in most advanced societies between "primitive moderns" and the new supporters of the proposition that individual desires of any kind should not be restrained by any sort of legal, moral, religious or societal bind as long as no damage is incurred by other people or, by extension, the environment. It is the case for example of same-sex marriages, all claims around biomedical research, and also absolute economic freedom like the right of each people to print her own currency.

In the real world, all these clashes intersect and interact adding to the confusion as they refer to incompatible resolution frameworks where conflicting parties can borrow from each other ideas and other means to prevail but cannot really find a common ground for negotiation. This is typically the case of fundamentalist terrorism that uses the latest technology to pursue its attacks or conversely modern democracies recurring to selective killings without any form of trial and justifying this on purely sacrificial grounds ("it is better for one to die for the rest to be saved"). Far from what Samuel Huntington predicted, the world at the beginning of the 21st century cannot be read simply as a clash of well-defined civilizations, as actually each civilization is to some extent fractured from within by multiple, incompatible and irresolvable modes of mimetic behavior and hence conflict.

Mimetic theory provides a framework for understanding both ancient, sacrificial conflicts and the conflicts of the new post-modern world. What's more, mimetic theory challenges both main flavors of the current political thought that is liberalism and socialism.

Mimetic theory reverses the optimism of Hegel, and shows that there is no end to human competition as this will continue to the end of mankind. At the same time, it demonstrates that the State is yet another superstition that must be deconstructed in the path to the end of history (which, at least according to Girard, has a high chance of ending up in apocalyptic self-destruction). And yet, no being is as social as man, as people move forward only through imitation and cannot escape the "wisdom of crowds". Liberalism, on the other hand, can embrace the vision of man as a competitive being, and might somehow concede that competition poses risks that have to be managed by a lean state focused on the prevention of violence and conflict. However, it can hardly accept that there is basically no such thing as an "independent rational individual", as two individuals would immediately start imitating each other desires, or their most intimate essence.

Mimetic theory, due to its ambiguous transcendentalist and materialist reading, can also help bridging the gap in the ever increasing conflict between religious and radically non-religious thought. But if mimetic theory can help establish a new cultural framework, what practical means can be adopted to help contain the multiple conflicts between individuals, individuals and society and at the largest scale the states themselves? For individuals (both considered as single ones and as groups with similar core interests and aspirations) the beginning of an answer could be in the broad notion of access as pointed out by Jeremy Rifkin. Desire can be restrained or at least managed if there are places where it can be satisfied and this place is in principle accessible to interested parties.

Conservative societies see the appearance of neighborhoods or even whole cities and states devoted to gaming, drugs but also plastic surgery and artificial insemination.

Regulated markets thrive in symbiosis with fiscal paradises where no regulation or at least much looser constraints are enforced. And conversely, liberal societies have to come to terms with groups that decide to commit themselves to non-liberal lifestyles, like the Amish in the United States or the growing conservative Muslim communities in European cities. The main problem with this approach is that to be truly effective it should somehow guarantee an opt-out/opt-in right to the individual, and that would often imply freedom of immigration between sovereign entities that are to say the least unwilling to grant this right.

However, modern conflicts since the end of World War 2 have implied the ever increasing growth of the number of refugees, that have gained an international legal status and immigration for economic reasons has become a global trend that affects all societies. If modernity has been defined by the mutual recognition of ethnic and geographic entities that shared a common belief in the sovereign state and the market economy and regulated the flow of trade and war while keeping people static in their respective cultural tradition, post modernity could be defined also by the mutual recognition of spiritual entities (in terms of homogeneous direction of desire), somehow tied but not necessarily identified with a geographic and sovereign entity that regulate the flow of people that choose to identify with them while keeping their ideal blueprint unchanged (or at least evolving with its own dynamics).

This would obviously not prevent conflicts from erupting, and they would most likely be of the worst species, the irresolvable one. With a bit more optimistic view than the one of Girard and Pascal, I believe that a growing comprehension of the dynamics of desire and sacrifice in political leadership and the general public can help restraint the rush to Armageddon (otherwise I would not be writing these booklets). A good example of leadership aware of the sense of self-sacrifice can be found in "Too Big to Fail", the insider account of the months that led to the demise of Lehman Brothers in September 2008, the near collapse of the global financial system and its rescue by the TARP program adopted in a hurry by the US Government. The story of the financial crisis is indeed full of mimetic behaviors and keywords (e.g. resentment, reputation, contagion, panic keep recurring throughout the book) and vivid examples of scapegoating. I would just recall the professional sacrifice of Joe Gregory, the Lehman Brothers executive vice president to buy his firm some breathing space and the voluntary humiliation that Secretary of Treasury and former Wall Street titan Henry Paulson, self-inflicted himself by kneeling in front of Democrat House Speaker Nancy Pelosi to save the TARP deal and probably the world economy in the middle of Congressional panic. A public educated in the dynamics of mimesis could be in a position to appreciate the providential step back and the turning of the other cheek that up to now in real world politics has been tantamount to failure.

Bibliography

"Civilization: West and The Rest" by Niall Ferguson (Paperback 2013)

"The Jewish Century" by Yuri Slezkine (Princeton University Press 2003)

"Red Cavalry" by Isaac Babel' (Penguin Classics 2003)

"Battling to the end: conversations with Benoit Chantre" by René Girard (Paperback 2009)

"Il potere che frena" by Massimo Cacciari (Adelphi 2013)

"Things hidden from the foundations of the world" by René Girard (Translated by S.Bann and M.Matteer)

"Violence and the Sacred" by René Girard (Translated by P.Gregory)

"Indifference and Envy: Anthropological analysis of the Modern economy" in "Contagion, 10-2003" by Paul Dumouchel

"Sacrifice and Envy: Liberalism and Social Justice" by Jean-Pierre Dupuy

"Introduction to the reading of Hegel" by A.Kojeve, R.Queneau, A.Bloom, J.Nichols

"Too Big To Fail" by Andrew Ross Sorkin, Viking Press 2009

Rival Brothers: A Mimetic View of East - West Relationships

"I tell you with certainty, tax collectors and prostitutes will get into God's kingdom ahead of you!" (Matthew, 21, 31)
"To God Belong the East and the West" (Quran, Surah of the Cow, v. 115)

Introduction

When back in 2005 I accepted to become the Sales support director for Turkey, Egypt and the Gulf countries, I had in the first place some second thoughts out of fear for travelling in a region that was widely known to be politically unstable, diverse and irremediably hostile to the average Western visitor. The very same feeling was echoed by friends who were reacting to the news like if I had told them I had some benign cancer and asked invariably if I was taking any special precautions when I was down there "in partibus infidelium".

Five years on, I have it very clear that the biggest risk we are facing in the West is simply not realizing that to the South and East of the Mediterranean there is a large and diversified civilization to which we are actually tied by thousands of years of mutual exchanges, and whose people share our very same goals of fulfilment in life while facing the very same challenges of re-assessing their identity in a world that changes with amazing speed. Sure, political stability is far away, there are objective dangers (I was in the Islamabad Marriott Hotel just three days before the attacks that claimed more than 200 lives) and many issues are entangled beyond imagination. Yet if we have to go anywhere we can only start from removing the "romantic myths" that, albeit comforting, keep ourselves prisoners of our own (mis-)representations and leave us in search for the next scapegoat, be it Osama Bin Laden, the Jewish lobby or the immigrant living next door.

The material herein contained has no claim of sociological, political, anthropological or even less theological or philosophical accuracy. Much if not all of it is likely to sound rather obvious to the expert eye. However, the target here is not to provide yet another brilliant idea, but rather a no-nonsense approach to the everyman when coming into contact with the "other side" of the Mediterranean over a beer or a cup of tea or, should one have the possibility, thoughts to be used in a television talk show, trying to popularize as much as possible the potent ideas of René Girard's Mimetic Theory. Short, it is a small contribution to what could be a "Cultural Lonely Planet Guide to Our Rivals", where rivals is used here in its original meaning of "the people living on the other side of the river".

The paper is structured as follows: In the first Chapter, by using some demographic data, literary examples and anecdotes, we will highlight how West and East are actually haunted by the very same set of identity and uncertainty problems each leading to a similar set of taboos and prejudices. In the second Chapter, mainly by recurring to some literary examples, we will show that there is indeed between the two worlds a much deeper level of understanding and interconnection whose dynamics can be explained by the mechanisms of mimetic theory. We will use here mostly the works of Miguel de Cervantes and Orhan Pamuk. Finally, in the third Chapter we will focus more on the approach guidelines, briefly explaining the three concepts that we have found useful when in the everyday dialogue with friends and colleagues the topic came to cultural issues.

The novelty here is maybe the appeal to the "merchant spirit" and the "open challenge" concept rather than the usual and in my opinion also somehow hypocritical notion of "tolerance". Throughout the paper, I will make an almost interchangeable use of the terms "West" and "East", "Europe" and "Middle East" (meaning the region spanning from North Africa to Iran and including the Arabian Peninsula) and "Christianity" and "Islam", knowing very well that they include a huge variety of people, civilizations, languages and cultures. However, there is no place like the Mediterranean where a relatively "easy" demarcation can be drawn between the North and South shores and at the same time the mutual influence has been so close that Western and Eastern people living along these coasts are by far the best entitled to act as bridges and ambassadors between these worlds.

Chapter 1 - Facing each other fears

If we put Europe and the Middle East in a broader geo-economic and cultural perspective stretching the last 60 years from the end of Word War II, we find an amazing level of structural similarities:

Sharing the same economic history and perspectives Both Europe and the Middle East had a post World War II economic boom that brought an historically unmatched development in the region, and this despite (or maybe also thanks to) 40 years of Cold War in Europe and all the conflicts that plagued the Middle East from the 1948 first Arab-Israel war to the last Iraqi war. For example, the story of the Bin Laden family, while horribly tainted by the deeds of Osama, is first and foremost the account of an extraordinary entrepreneurial saga from the founder Mohamed to the current leader Bakr. It has nothing to envy and indeed a lot in common when it comes to their relationship with political power with similar European industrial dynasties like the Agnelli in Italy or the Porsche in Germany. Both regions see a natural path ahead as financial and manufacturing stalwarts (Europe) or trade and natural resource hubs (Middle East), yet both have to manage radical changes (with their associated threats and opportunities) in their reference markets brought forward by rising powers like China, Russia and Brazil.

Sharing the same geopolitical risks In addition to that, both Europe and the Middle East face similar amounts of geopolitical uncertainty: each one of them is witnessing the seemingly unstoppable growth of Asian giant nations (i.e. China and India) next to the superpowers of yesterday, Russia and US, displacing the known and relatively comfortable and predictable system of alliances of Cold War times. Europe and Middle East are dealing with old and new rivalries that prevent the states of these regions to reach an adequate scale to effectively assert their interest and compete in the global arena of the 21st century, assuming there is one such thing as a "common European" or "common Middle Eastern" interest, which is still to be proven on a number of key items. As a result, both see their future development prospects or simply their existence as independent entities as not granted at all or at least uncertain.

Sharing the same cultural quakes Beside the economical and geopolitical similarities, Western and Eastern Mediterranean societies in the post-World War II era have undergone massive amounts of cultural change, both characterized by a general trend to challenge if not outright do away with the established traditions and social hierarchies. We can just recall here the Marxist and Socialist wave that peaked in the 1968 protests in Europe, mirrored by the Arab socialism ways of Nasser in Egypt and his fellow regimes in Syria and the Levant. Questioning of social structure and economic development led inevitably to an ever growing role and progressive emancipation for women that is still in full swing, albeit with very different speeds across different countries. Too much "left swing" also led to conservative reactions in both societies, reactions that had nonetheless to take the new into account: so while the West saw the Roman Catholic Church re-discuss its approach to many themes and rely on a number of loosely organized "ecclesial movements" to re-assert its views within a secular society, in a rather similar way a number of Muslim movements are trying to re-adapt themselves and Middle Eastern societies to the changed circumstances.

Just as example, pressure from the modern banking system led to Islamic Finance and you can hardly find a single booklet of Islamic proselytism that does not try to find also some "scientific" background to confirm the correctness of Islam. Finally, from a political point of view, Turkey makes for an excellent example: after a sweeping secular revolution that transformed the remnants of the Ottoman Empire into modern Turkey with changes so substantial that not even the French Revolution dared to attempt it is now openly giving more public space to religious beliefs and habits (Ataturk in the 1920s changed at once calendar, law, system of government, official administrative language and alphabet while French revolutionaries failed to replace Latin alphabet with something else). But make no mistake, despite the sinister crypto-fundamentalist image that some media like to depict the Turkish AKP party it actually looks much more like the Muslim equivalent of Christian Democrat parties and indeed reports of how AKP members and sympathizers like to behave recall almost perfectly the descriptions of the "Democrazia Cristiana" politicians made immortal by the Sicilian writer Leonardo Sciascia in his short novel "Todo Modo".

Sharing the same wave of immigration Publicly available data on the World Bank web site, show the percentage of immigration in some of the richest and influential EU and Mideast countries as of 2005. It is apparent that the relative percentage of migrants to the total population are far higher in Middle East (ranging from more than 25% in Saudi Arabia to over 80% in Qatar) than in the rest of Europe, that barely goes beyond 10% in the biggest countries to reach 22% only in Switzerland. The rates in Western Europe are now substantially aligned to those of the US, while in many Middle Eastern countries the rates are way higher of those of countries like Australia that are still pursuing a "growth by immigration" policy. While we read every day in European papers about the danger (or opportunity, depending if you read far right or far left publications) that immigration might one day change European culture for good, we almost never read at least in widespread media channels that Mid Eastern countries face the same tidal wave of immigration from places as culturally disparate as the Philippines or China, not to mention the consistent amount of Western expatriates that make up the ranks of middle and senior management of many firms.

In the streets of Riyadh it is not uncommon to notice advertisements written in Sanskrit by mobile phone companies targeting the large Indian community. The only papers I recall on Mid Eastern immigration in Western papers protested against the strict immigration rules being enforced in the Gulf countries (like e.g. mandatory HIV tests) but one has to wonder what measures EU states would undertake under the pressure of public opinion if ever faced with immigration rates of more than 50%. US citizens in the aftermath of 9/11 attacks accepted restrictions to civil liberties for the sake of national security, and the latest debate ongoing around body scans at airports shows the trend is still very much in place. And it is maybe not at all a coincidence that one of the most discussed restrictions in terms of immigration religious freedom, the so called "Minaret Ban" in Switzerland, popped up in the European country with the highest immigration rate. If you then go to small talk conversation in front of a beer in Western Europe or a shisha house in the Middle East, almost invariably you will land on the argument of the "evil sheikhs belonging to Al-Qaeda" organizing immigrant trade to destroy Europe identity or, in perfect mirroring, the "evil Jewish lobby" trying to do the same to the Arab and Muslim world.

Sharing the same envy Mimetic theory has taught us a lot about the central role of envy in Western culture and literature, and one has just to look at René Girard works for a detailed analysis. Western societies are to some extent huge machines where people are pushed to crave other people possessions and conversely show off whatever they can to have others crave for one's own possessions. This role of envy is indeed very well known in the East, with the difference that most of moral prescriptions, accepted behaviors and even the laws are indeed targeted at preventing envy from happening rather than at enticing it like in the West. While this might seem a capital difference, it is actually the flip side of the mimetic crisis. The West is in full ritual mode to reproduce the mimetic crisis, the East puts the focus on the prohibition side trying to prevent a new crisis from happening.

To explain the concept, I will refer to Saudi Arabia which has one of the most conservative societies of Middle East and to Rajaa Al-Sanea's book "Girls of Riyadh" which describes the lives of four upper class Saudi girls in the years between high school and graduation. The girls go through all the romance and enchantments of love and passion, and as it always happens not every story turns out well: one of the girls gets to a happy marriage, another to a sad divorce, another one again gets disappointed in love and seeks some form of fulfillment in work. As the book is filled with the description of Saudi society habits, it has been hailed in the West as yet another proof of how Saudi society mistreats and oppresses women, and I am afraid it has been banned in Saudi Arabia for the very same reasons. After all, Saudi society is going through a development and learning curve that for example would require France to go from Charlemagne to Charles de Gaulle in just four generations.

However, if you take out the rituals of Saudi society, the stories could very well belong to four girls located in Paris or London that grow up, get a good education at university, get to know boys of their age and then life develops itself for the better or the worse. Reading the book carefully and complementing it with some real life experience of Saudi society lets a deeper truth emerge, that is women having to wear "abayas" are actually a consequence of a much broader attempt to block any possible source of malicious glances that might trigger others' envy. Family relationships, space allocation in public places like restaurants and shopping malls, the rhythm of social life is indeed paced on the need to prevent intrusions from the outside that might create insane desires, a chatter of gossip too much and eventually break the so much difficult to find and therefore precious harmony within the family or between the families. Only trusted individuals can be progressively and cautiously be introduced though the various circles that defend the family privacy. Yet the pressure to stand out among the others finds eventually some outlets that are deemed socially acceptable like fancy cars or privileged mobile numbers or, as I learned, having your name carved on a knife hang in public at a top class restaurant. As mimetic theory tells, when it comes to imitating desires and creating envy, the object does not ultimately matter much so if you hide women desire will stick eventually to something else.

Sharing the same political (r-)evolution dynamics If we look back at the past few months in North Africa, it is impossible not to draw a direct comparison between the hugely popular and relatively peaceful uprisings of Egypt and Tunisia that led to the toppling of long-standing and seemingly very entrenched regimes and their counterparts in Central and Eastern Europe at the end of 1980s and most recently in Ukraine in 2004 (another revolution that was followed by a similar uprising in Lebanon). Comparisons range from the surprise and speed of the uprising, the weak response of the ruling governments and the contagion effect that led to the victory of the revolt. Sure, there is also plenty of differences in the context, ways and outcomes that the political changes in Tunisia and Egypt will lead with respect to the Central European precedents and this paper does not even dare start a sketch of analysis. Yet one cannot remark the stunning resemblance between the Central European and North African non-violent revolutions.

Even where things are going in the wrong direction like in Libya, one cannot avoid recalling the violent meltdown of Yugoslavia, where a general but not compact hostility against the regime mixed with conflicting external interests and a fragmented ethnic and religious societal texture led to a bloody stalemate. Finally, we cannot but recall that also in violence and warfare the two sides of the Mediterranean have been engaged in mutual imitation: terrorism in its modern form was actually invented in the early 1800s by Spaniards that were waging their irregular war ("guerilla") on French and Turkish troops to which Napoleon had outsourced the control of Spain as the bulk of the French Army' was busy in Central Europe. When Carl Schmitt first described the new concept of asymmetric war in its "Theory of Partisan" work with its implications, he could not yet fathom that the very same dynamics would be at work in Iraq 200 years later than Napoleon and with Turkish troops replaced by an array of private security contractors that would nonetheless lead to the same escalation of limitless violence and brutality.

So here is the reality we have to face: due to the uncontrollable forces of history, on both sides of the Mediterranean, our societies and we have been more and more exposed to a giant scale mimetic crisis, with growing amounts of disillusion, resentment and fear. What's worse, the economic and political environment is far more uncertain and unstable to make sure these tensions and stress are kept under control. As we know from mimetic theory, society and individuals under mimetic stress tend to find a solution by looking for scapegoats. No wonder that immigrants and the "other side" in general come in as handy first candidates, with Muslim in the West and Christians in the East being increasingly subject to subtle discriminations or in the most apparent cases outright prosecution, restriction of civil rights and terror attacks. But we know that this is no solution, because it hides the basic reality that violence is from within us. So before moving on to discuss how to try to defuse it, let's look back first and see that indeed, some of the most enlightened men on both sides already had found what we are now trying to re-assert.

Chapter 2 - The Romanesque Truth versus the Romantic Lie

Interestingly, these underlying similarities had been already spotted in literature where there seems to be a "Romanesque" cultural truth of mutual similarities and interconnection that surpasses the "romantic" view of the "clash of civilization" supporters. I would like here to draw just a few examples from literature that, read in the perspective of Mimetic theory, show how brilliant novelists have indeed been able to grasp a truth still unknown in many "think tanks". Let's start intentionally from one of the most famous examples of clash, namely the Turkish-European conflict that led to the battle of Lepanto in 1571.

By just using a few literary references we show that the clash of civilization theorem has a lot of flaws. We will use as sources "The Last Crusader" by Louis de Wohl and "Altai" by Wu Ming. "The Last Crusader" by Louis de Wohl, is a novel dedicated to the life of Don Juan of Austria and gives a clearly apologetic and romantic view of the conflict. The storyboard looks ready for a Hollywood movie about the good Christians and the evil Turks, yet in the narrative some cracks appear: the author reports of continuous fights between Venetian sailors and Spanish soldiers on the way to the battle, with Spanish troopers regularly being hung by Venetian officers for insubordination. The least one can say there was no general consensus on the West side on how to address the enemy. And the explanation is readily given: Venice did not believe at all in the need of an additional challenge and thought that there was some room of negotiations with the Ottoman Empire after the defeat of Famagosta.

In "Altai", we get some more insight: the real problem for the Ottomans was to hide the fact that the recent victory at Famagosta had indeed been a half defeat as the till then invincible Turkish Army had been blocked for months with huge losses by a well designed fortress and a small garrison of Venetians. But a defeat was needed for the Ottoman Empire to negotiate a peace and a defeat at sea, where Venetians where known for their mastery, would not raise suspects. And indeed, after the battle the far more powerful reasons of trade led to a quick peace. Miguel de Cervantes took active part in the battle, bearing for the rest of his life the consequences of the wounds he received. But, despite his taking very clear sides, he never conceded to the clash of civilization rhetoric.

If we look at the "Don Quijote", we discover with respect to the theme of the Mediterranean rivalry an attitude as illuminating as the one he shows about desire in other parts of his masterpiece. First of all, the whole novel is built on a narrative technique that lets a Moor author, Sidi Ermete Benengeli, be the source of the story of the Most Christian Knight Don Quijote, creating a fictional trick by which the model of modern Western roman is indeed an Arabic tale. Then, three entire chapters (39 to 41) are dedicated to the history of the escape from Algiers of Ruy Perez de Viedma, a Spanish prisoner that brings with him a beautiful Moorish woman that has secretly converted to Christianity. Cervantes embedded many autobiographical notes in this tale, nonetheless it brings such a huge amount of detail that some more analysis is helpful.

In the first part of the tale in Chapter 39, Cervantes provides the geopolitical picture of the Mediterranean between 1567 and 1580, clearly mentioning the multifaceted nature of the conflict and adding lots of insight into the political entanglement of the time: first, the reluctance of Genoa to take part to the war against the Ottoman Empire (only 3 ships sent) not to help too much Venice reclaim its power in the Eastern Mediterranean, in addition to the open alliance of France with the Sultan to oppose Spain. Against the infidels yes, but up to a point.

Second, the multinational nature of the Ottoman armies: Cervantes correctly states the Italian nationality of Uluc Ali, whose fleet alone survived at Lepanto and then became head of the Ottoman fleet. A clear understanding of Ottoman hierarchies: the head of the Fleet is correctly reported as third most important rank in the Ottoman Empire after Grand Vizier and Mufti. Interestingly enough, we add that the Grand Vizier at the time of Lepanto, Sokollu Mehmet Pasha, was a Serbian Janissary that made the entire career to the highest spot. His brother, on the other hand, became the Patriarch of the Orthodox Church in the Ottoman Empire.

Third, a very detailed military analysis on the troubles of Ottoman infantry in dealing with modern European fortresses: the battle for the re-conquest of Tunis (openly criticized by Cervantes as a hopeless stronghold with no military meaning) cost Ottoman forces more than 20.000 casualties out of an army of 50.000 to overcome a garrison of less than 7000 opponents that suffered around 3000 losses. A 7:1 loss ratio to claim a win is in military terms a Pyrrhus victory at best. And exactly when the battle rages in Tunis, a small note tells that, a few kilometers away, the coastal town of Tabarka quietly continues to be managed by the Genoese Republic that exploits its reefs for coral fishing. This maybe is a favor returned by Ottomans to Genoa for sending just three ships to Lepanto, nonetheless it can be explained by Mimetic theory but certainly not by the clash of civilization approach.

After this scene setting, in Chapters 40 and 41 the story moves to the personal adventures of Ruy de Viedma and his fellow prisoners. Here again, a careful reading shows details that are all but disturbing for the supporters of the clash of civilization point of view: Christian prisoners are generally well treated, except under the rule of Hassan Ali, a Venetian renegade whose ferocity shocks Turks first. Then, prisoners do have pen and paper readily available to write home to get their relatives to pay the ransom, and the harbour of Algiers hosts both pirate ships and Spanish vessels doing regular trade with Spanish cities. And Christian prisoners can talk to Muslim women in a way that Cervantes itself defines as "way too liberal", at least for XVII century Spain. Things seem more difficult between Moors and Turks, whose hostility is depicted in a number of episodes and openly put in parallel (by Moors!) to the one existing between French and Spaniards.

In this context, Ruy and his comrades get in touch with Zahara, the Muslim daughter of the richest man of Algiers that secretly converted to Christianity thanks to the devotion to the Virgin Mary taught to her by an old Christian servant. She now wants to go to Spain and gives the prisoners all the money needed to finance their ransom and buy a boat. In architecting the escape a key role is played by an unnamed Spanish renegade that wants actually to come back to Spain and is collecting from Christians certificates of fair treatment to help defend his case in front of the Holy Inquisition back in homeland Spain. The fact that there is a technical term ("Tornadizo") and a clear judicial procedure for this category leads to think that this is far from an isolated case and again, it badly matches with the romantic clash of civilization picture where renegades would deserve only horrible death, repented or not. The conversion of the Moorish girl also leaves some doubts: she constantly references Lela Marien, that is the Virgin Mary, and Allah, but never makes any explicit reference to Jesus, the Holy Ghost, or anything else with a clear theological Christian characteristic. Also, as soon as she lands in Spain, she asks to enter a Church to adore the pictures representing Mary, and although some of these paintings might well have represented the Nativity or Crucifixion, no mention of Jesus is found here as well. Knowing that Islam has strong similarity to Roman Catholicism when it comes to Mary (including virginal conception of Jesus) one wonders if Zahara really converted to Christianity or is rather pursuing a somehow unorthodox version of Islam, more tolerated in Roman Catholic Spain. With a telling mistake, when asked about Trinity, many Muslims name actually the Father, Jesus and the Virgin Mary!

Finally, the prisoners manage to escape and the only serious risk of their journey is represented not by Moors sent to pursue them but rather by a French pirate ship that, crossed at night just off the coast of Malaga, immediately fires artillery at the fugitives refusal to identify themselves. The French captain stops just short of throwing the company to sharks, leaving them instead on a small boat at the mercy of the waves. Cervantes ends with the remark that the crew was from Britanny and was in a hurry to get back to La Rochelle, the haven of French Protestants.

Almost four centuries later, the Turkish writer and Nobel prize winner Orhan Pamuk keeps coming back to the theme of mutual influence and interconnection. We will mention just two books, "My name is Red" and "The White Castle". In "My name is Red', everything is around imitation: for the 1000th anniversary of the Hajira, the Sultan wants to donate to the

Venetian ambassador a book depicted by the best miniaturists of the Palace showing all the achievements of the Ottoman Empire centered around a portrait of the Sultan himself painted in the way Ottomans have seen the Venetians paint themselves.

The top three palace miniaturists are selected to decorate the various scenes in a work surrounded by great secrecy, but competition to draw the Sultan portrait, the core of the book, triggers immediate envy between them that eventually leads one of them to start a chain of murders to seize the portrait. Black is the detective charged to find the killer and the main character of the book. He is himself entangled in a love rivalry for the daughter of the editor of the book, Sekure, who lost her husband at war, and not in the Lepanto battle, but, as Pamuk notes, in the campaigns against the Ottomans archrivals, the Persians. The symmetry with the French and Spanish episode narrated by Cervantes could not be more apparent. So the widow is now contended between Black and Hasan, her brother-in-law, that since the time his brother married Sekure deeply envies his late brother and wants to marry the widow. Probably not even René Girard himself could have imagined a plot where imitation of mutual desires for love, celebrity and power intertwine so much! I recall here just two examples where the role of mutual imitation is described and even theorized in almost metaphysical terms.

The first one is the dialogue between the Sultan and the editor of the book that served also as ambassador to Venice, at the end of Chapter 20. The editor vividly describes to the Sultan how the passion for portraits in Venice spread like an epidemic with all the rich and powerful rushing to have their faces depicted. What are Venetians looking for into portraits? The answer of the ambassador is simple: to stay forever in front of us, to tell each other that they exist and that they are unique and different from all the others. Pure mimetic models, in Girardian terms. And the ambassador cannot escape the spell: he feels he would better understand his own meaning in the world, if only he would be portrayed like Venetian artists do. Frightened by his own desires, he resolves to put the magic power of the portrait at the service of the Ottoman Empire, and proposes the Sultan to have him portrayed and use his portrait to extend his influence over Christian powers. Initially, the Sultan dismisses the whole idea: despite all the good intentions, portraits would inevitably turn themselves into idols, their existence becoming independent of the original model. The account ends with a masterpiece note: "For this reason, said the Sultan, I cannot accept to have myself portrayed in a painting". "But he really wanted it", whispered the Ambassador with a Satanic smile".

The monologue of Satan in Chapter 47 is the Devil self-defense to precisely refute the argument that trying to paint the way Venetians paint (and hence the drive to imitate Western habits) is nothing but yet another devilish temptation. To make his point, Satan refers directly to the Quran. According to the Muslim Holy Book (e.g. Surah of the Limb et al.), Satan is expelled from Paradise not for openly rebelling against God but rather for disobeying Him when God asked him and all the other angels to adore the newly created Adam. Satan refuses to bow on the ground that the new creature is made out of clay and not fire like angels and hence it is inferior. Subtly, Satan seems to imply that he is "more right than God" in supporting his refusal to bow to Adam as he is more adherent to the order of the Creation than the Creator Himself. As Satan goes on, the fact is that Adam (and therefore all mankind) was granted by God the adoration of inherently superior beings and hence man could only develop an attitude to seek adoration, appraisal and at least respect by his peers and subjects. So imitation is dismissed by Satan as a temptation of his own making, but recast as the core mechanism embedded in mankind since its beginning. Of course, Satan does not mention that beyond his refusal to bow there might well have been envy for the new creature and the attempt of imitating God by trying to be "righter than Him" in using the elemental hierarchy argument.

If the line of defense chosen by Satan is correct, then the drive to create mimetic idols through imitation is actually part of God plan, quite a big dilemma. But if we instead believe that this is not true and somehow Satan is lying to prepare us yet another trap, then we have the issue that the parts of the Muslim Holy Scripture support his claim and we are left with the even bigger dilemma of figuring out how this is possible. Leaving aside theology and sticking to the literary and anthropological side of the story, the monologue of Satan captures the ambivalence of mimesis as engine of positive and negative interaction, social and political driver of all orders and disorders.

The other novel of Orhan Pamuk dedicated to the mutual exchange between West and East is "The White Castle". It is entirely based on the history of the relationship between an Italian scientist captured by Turkish pirates and eventually ended up as aide of one of the top astronomers and scientist of the Sultan court. The two scientists start to learn from each other, they help fight together a plague that bursts in Istanbul and help the Sultan develop a new war machine that should be used to win over the European fortresses that prevent the further expansion of the Empire. After a decades long work the machine is ready and as the war erupts between the Turkish empire and Poland the two scientists follow the Sultan army to the "White Castle", that is the fortress that protects the Polish borders. There is no detail on the battle outcome, but the result is that eventually the two scientists swap clothes and while the Turkish astronomer goes to Italy the Italian one stays in Istanbul taking his place in a perfect mimetic exchange.

To remind us that mimesis is always at work Pamuk openly quotes Cervantes in the figure of a Spanish prisoner (a short "cameo" in movie language) that wants to imitate his compatriot. What's more, the whole narrative style of the novel is a monologue of the Italian scientist with high dramatization of the dialogues and a relatively scant lack of descriptive detail to make the setting as abstract as possible. The very same approach had been followed by another Spaniard, Miguel de Unamuno, in his short novel "Abel Sanchez" dedicated to the theme of envy at the dawn of the Spanish Civil War in 1928.

Chapter 3 – A Mimetic Theory for the Everyman?

Using as example two prominent authors belonging to different sides and ages of the Mediterranean I tried to demonstrate that the mimetic nature of the relationship has been apparent to the brightest spirits on the two sides. But if this was fine in a world where masses basically did not had a chance to establish daily links and lived most of their lives in their own relatively isolated communities, it is no longer enough today where mutual exposure to other cultures has increased dramatically as well as the amount of damage that anyone can inflict thanks to the advances of technology. One finds on the Internet videos of René Girard conferences and speeches as well as instructions on how to build rudimentary bombs, so we need to develop ideas that can be used on both sides to spread the "Cervantes & Pamuk" fruitful understanding of mimesis rather than the nefarious "Bush vs Bin Laden" one.

Ideally, the best way would be to have classes about mimetic theory in all high schools and we might well end up there over the next few decades however we can start working in that direction with maybe a more immediate approach. To do so, I think we can leverage on three key concepts, that is tradition, respect and challenge, already well known on both sides of this sea.

Tradition: our "default configuration" to make sense of the world Let me introduce this by recalling the vivid memory of a young professor of religion in my youth in the highly politicized atmosphere of the state high schools of the 1980s in Italy. Climate was such that the hour of religious education almost invariably ended up in free-speech debates where the teacher basically kept spending his weekly hour of lecture answering more or less malicious questions around politics, history and morality from the classroom. One day, the topic "du jour" turned to tradition, with the classroom obviously pushing the idea that tradition was but a bunch of old ideas to be quickly dismissed if we ever wanted to embrace modernity and progress. Much to the surprise of the audience, the teacher actually said that tradition be better considered as any set of knowledge, beliefs and behaviors that every individual could not avoid being proposed by his/her environment to make sense of reality and start navigating his/her own journey in this world. And as during the journey these beliefs and evidences would be put to test, every individual would invariably modify to some extent this body of knowledge and attitude and re-transmit it to his/her descendants in a slightly modified way. If this is the definition, one student implied, then a Communist family should bring up their babies as Communists. His very consequential answer was: "Yes, absolutely".

25 years since that moment, I have not yet found a better definition. Whether we like it or not, we come up with a more or less defined set of values and beliefs. We can't but use these tools to move in reality but as much as we would be insane to prejudicially look down on them, we need to recognize when they no longer serve us and we have to modify them before passing them on. So how does that translate in dealing with our rivals? Simply into recognizing that awkward or unacceptable behaviors in another tradition have probably valid backgrounds behind, and before indulging into an easy contempt, judgment must be constantly applied. At the same time, this is no excuse for going into easy relativism where anything can be justified on historical or cultural grounds: if we face more and more the same challenges we will have to look at each other tools and inevitably modify them to cope with the ever changing environment.

"Girls of Riyadh" again gives a good example of this process at work. The four upper class Saudi girls of different cultural backgrounds in the key age between 15 and 25, show how core choices around vision of oneself and how to lead life are typically taken in mutual influence with the surrounding environment. Lamees is coming from a liberal Lebanese family and during high school time is by far the most provocative and outspoken, smuggling forbidden videotapes into high school. With the due proportions, she would typically smoke marijuana and have free sex in a Western setting. But again, it is structures rather than specific individual actions that matter here. Then we have Gamrah, fully conservative and aligned with family traditions, she accepts a combined family marriage as soon as she is out of high school. Michelle falls in in love and seeks to marry Faisal, a Saudi boy whose family ultimately opposes the marriage as the mother of Michelle is American and the father, although Muslim and occupying a very good social position, is not coming from the Saudi establishment. Finally, Sadeem is traditional in her will to form a perfect family and yet too explicit in the way she approaches boys, that are at once attracted and scared by her. Going through life, they all come to change their initial stance in response to circumstances and events: Lamees becomes a family mother model, starting to wear the veil even in relatively more liberal Jeddah. Gamrah, unfairly divorced by her husband that leaves her alone with her newborn kid, rejects a further proposal for marriage that would require her to leave her kid with her parents, challenging the will of her whole family. Michelle eventually opts for her Western side, showing up at Faisal marriage to mock her former boyfriend indecisiveness and eventually leaves the country to go working in Dubai.

Consciously or not, traditions are influenced by circumstances, events and morph over time with the people, irrespective of their will or the will of the society surrounding them. All the better then to critically propose a set of traditional values, where critically here means literally giving evidence of the historical, religious, cultural and other reasons that led to a certain set of beliefs leaving the door open to change them and motivate the reasons that led to drop a certain set of values/behaviors, modify others and create new ones. Short, the process would take place anyway, in only a more unconscious and painful way. Then, better manage the changes in the open in full transparency.

Respect This is nowadays a somehow abused word that way too often means "Turn your eye the other way, behave calmly and hide your contempt in public". If you have to continue the exercise for a long time or the circumstances are particularly disturbing to your beliefs, it becomes "Tolerance". No wonder it does not work, as it is trapped in the "Me good you evil" scheme. To try to overcome this, we should go back to the Latin etymology, that is the verb "respicere" which holds the two key ingredients of "looking at the other" with the "re" prefix that conveys at once the reflection back to us of our staring and our turning behind to look over our shoulder. In other words, I look at the other and by looking at the other I cannot help turning my eye back to me and wonder "Am I facing the same issues he is facing? And what ways have I come up to deal with it? And how come they are at times so strikingly different and so strikingly similar? And, let's admit it, for all his diversity, is there maybe something that I actually admire him and I would like to be it myself?" All of a sudden, easy recipes disappear and one is more and more led to question his own tradition rather than the others. After all, Voltaire made it very clear that there was no real

106

tolerance without this painful rationalization of diversity, without the journey and the overcoming of the hatred of the other which is revealing our own dark side. In mimetic vocabulary, our own scandal.

The concept is closely knit to the one of tradition: the more people adhere to a well-defined set of core values, the more they understand those of others. Conversely, the more the adherence stops at the formal aspects, the more a different culture is seen as a danger. The same dynamics makes all empires at the peak of their power develop much more open and tolerant societies than those of smaller nations.

<u>Challenge</u> So far, we highlighted the value of one's tradition and the need to keep constantly an eye on ourselves while evaluating other cultures and traditions. Now, how to make sure that the relationship that establishes between the parties is a fruitful one? I suspect that far too often the calls to "dialogue" actually hide a "double monologue", and the frank confrontation of ideas and visions is avoided somehow out of fear of conflict. But this is a losing position, as mimetic theory tells us that resentment will continue to build up and eventually burst into worse forms. I believe it is more useful to adopt an open challenge approach, where challenge here is meant primarily in its trade meaning. Merchants and traders (not to mention bankers and financiers!) have never been the darlings of priests and philosophers, often accused (and not without merit) to put money and business in front of everything else. But, as J.P. Dupuy remarked in "Envy and Sacrifice", markets contain mimetic mechanisms in the double sense of "embedding them" and "manage to limit their risks of escalation". Indeed, market actors have the privilege of living in a highly mimetic environment, as for example it is vividly represented in "Too Big to Fail", the journalistic account of the Lehman Brothers crisis of 2008. The book is indeed full of mimetic behaviors and keywords (e.g. resentment, reputation, contagion, panic keep recurring throughout the text) as well as apparent examples of corporate scapegoating like the sacrificial firing of Lehman Brothers no.2 executive Joe Gregory to buy Lehman some breathing space at the beginning of the crisis or the voluntary humiliation that Secretary of Treasury Hank Paulson self-

inflicted himself by kneeling in front of Speaker of the House Nancy Pelosi and all Congressmen to save the TARP deal and the world economy in the middle of Congressional panic.

All is then bad and these people are irremediably lost to their mimetic hypnosis that brings us from an asset bubble to another? As a sales person aware of mimetic theory, I would like to instead say something definitely in praise of the "market approach" applied to intercultural relationship, to some extent trying to develop on the key remarks of René Girard, seen of course from an "insider perspective". No matter the cultural background, marketers tend to develop remarkable mimetic qualities if they want to survive and thrive in their environment:

First, strong sense of the counterparty and how it might behave or react, be it a customer or a competitor. You are not a good market and sales person if you do not keep asking yourself and tune your action to what customers and competitors want and how they might react. It's a constant exercise of putting oneself in someone else's shoes.

Second, they see the competitor as a "iustus hostis", exactly in the sense that Carl Schmitt highlighted in his works about the origins of international law. Competition is tough, as they want to steal your customers and sales away from you. At the same time, without them you would not be able to properly articulate your own proposition so there would be no market. And as much as markets can be very hard at times, I have never met a real salesman that would be willing to trade the market game with a quiet life.

Third, traders know that competing is a game where you have to continuously imitate and differentiate, with successful models constantly swapping roles with the imitating rivals. Launch a new product, win a market one day and the day after your competitors will be copying you with some slight differences you will careful pay attention to, because one of them could be the next great idea that you might have to copy (with a slight change, of course) the year after. And eventually, traders know that challenge never stops and that after all the ups and the unavoidable downs it makes for an ever better marketplace.

A prominent Stanford graduate like Peter Thiel openly acknowledged the value mimetic theory brought to his job of starting up companies where loosely defined roles can lead to conflicts. We just recall that one of those startups is Facebook. Mutually, can we adopt market attitudes into tackling cultural issues involving cultures, values and religion? After all, a strong trade culture is present since time immemorial on both sides of the Mediterranean. The expression of "supermarket of religion" or, to that matter, "supermarket of cultures" has been around for a while and I have always found it evoked in a somehow negative meaning, as to underline the complete "commodification" of culture, the last stage of the capitalist evolution in the Marxist view. However, markets in the Mediterranean have existed long before the birth of capitalism, and mimetic laws governing them date back even further to the origins of culture, at least according to Mimetic theory.

I would therefore put it in a more positive perspective, recasting the market as the place where originally goods are proposed for sale by traders to their potential buyers in the midst of competition by other traders. So the first point is, be proud of your goods (be them philosophies, morals or religion) and try to sell them in the right way. Second, watch out for competition, study them carefully and be prepared to compete in a fair way, by means of mutual challenge. As you cannot escape the mimetic mechanism, all the better to embrace it and play by its rules. On a personal basis, I can report that the amount of respect you get (and you in turn grant) from people belonging to different cultures is proportional to how openly you play your identity, be it the one of a Christian, a Muslim, a Jew or an outright Atheist born in any of these environments.

And this respect only grows when you openly and frankly engage in mutual cultural challenge, with for example, yourself providing background of why we in the West strongly believe in State and Religion separation and your friend in the East pointing out to the countless text contradictions in the Bible that would be solved by the Quranic reading. People would not generally change ideas or religion, but for sure mutual understanding increases, following exactly the same dynamics by which in healthy markets you tend to grow a respect of your competitors (and you might occasionally go working for them if the right conditions arise!).

Conclusion - *In praise of the merchant spirit*

I am persuaded that, despite all the bloodshed and violence that the Mediterranean has witnessed, impure and mundane trading is indeed one of the key forces that kept the relationships alive and allowed rival civilizations to continue influencing each other in a positive way. I like to think that Jesus was also referring to this dynamics when He said "Tax collectors and prostitutes will precede you in the Kingdom of Heaven". Tax officers had a reputation between fellow Jews no better than the one of a Wall Street banker today. Yet, unlike Pharisees who kept hiding from themselves the truth of being prosecutors with their supposed purity, the tax collectors' connection and engagement with the Roman counterpart put them at an advantage in understanding the mimetic game. And guess what? For a long period of his life, Miguel de Cervantes served as a tax collector for the fleet of the Spanish monarchy. As René Girard himself declared that there cannot be an external point of view of mutual imitation as we are all constantly part of it, for the good or the worse, we better learn from the rules used by the impure and despised and try to build our way to Heaven rather than try to be purest and quickly pave our way to Hell.

Bibliography

René Girard "La voix meconnue du reel" Grasset 2002 (Adelphi it.tr.)

Andrew Ross Sorkin "Too Big to Fail" Viking 2009

Orhan Pamuk "My name is Red" (It.tr. Einaudi 2001)

Orhan Pamuk "The White Castle"(It.tr. Einaudi 2005)

Miguel de Cervantes "Don Quijote" (It. tr. BUR 2009)

Louis de Wohl "The Last Crusader" (It.tr. BUR 2003)

Rajaa Al Sanea "Girls of Riyadh" Penguin Books 2008

Steve Coll "The Bin Ladens" Penguin Books 2009

Miguel de Unamuno "Abel Sanchez" Alianza Editorial 2004

Interview with Peter Thiel "http://www.youtube.com/watch?v=esk7W9Jowtc"

J.P. Dupuy "Sacrifice and Envy – Liberalism and Social Justice" (It.tr. ECIG 1997)

Wu Ming "Altai" Einaudi 2010

Carl Schmitt "The nomos of the Earth" (It.tr. Adelphi 1991)

Carl Schmitt "Theory of the Partisan" (It.tr. Adelphi 2005)

Acknowledgments

To Sherif, Hikmat, Othman, Mahmoud, Amjad, Idrees, Nazmiye, Emine, Ersin, Canberk, Sevket, Engin, Muniba, Shady, Sameh, Nagui, Rima, Dorsaf, Issam, Turki, the many Mohameds and all the others that placed the roots of this paper in a living relationship and not only in just yet another theory. To Enrico, that first mentioned to me "I see Satan falling like the Lightning" and effectively got me started on Mimetic theory. To my father, that long before he passed away he had already collected many Girard books in his library for me to continue on his readings. And most important, to my wife Alessandra and my kids, that had the patience of bearing with me as I spent many hours of my free time to put together this account.

About the Author

Luca Luchesini graduated in Telecom Networks Engineering from Politecnico di Milano in 1994 and has been working in multinational companies ever since.

He started self-learning Mimetic theory in 2007 by reading all major works of René Girard. In 2011, he published a paper about West and Middle East relationship at the annual Girardian COV&R conference 2011 dedicated to "Order/Disorder in History and Politics".

He can be reached at luca.luchesini@libero.it

www.ingramcontent.com/pod-product-compliance
Lightning Source LLC
Chambersburg PA
CBHW070539290526
45790CB00002B/559